SOUTH LONDON MURDERS

This is dedicated to the memory of my mother
Claire de Loriol
1911–1991
who imbued me with a love of reading

SOUTH LONDON MURDERS

Peter de Loriol

First published in 2007 by
Sutton Publishing Limited

Reprinted in 2008 by
The History Press
The Mill, Brimscombe Port,
Stroud, Gloucestershire, GL5 2QG
www.thehistorypress.co.uk

British Library Cataloguing in Publication Data
A catalogue record for this book is available from the British Library.

ISBN 978-0-7509-4426-7

Typeset in 10.5/13.5pt Sabon.
Typesetting and origination by
Sutton Publishing Limited.
Printed and bound in England.

CONTENTS

ACKNOWLEDGEMENTS

My grateful thanks to Janey, my wonderful wife, for her incisive comments on my punctuation, and to Sarah Hodgson, editor-in-chief, *SW Magazine*, for her continued support.

Thanks for their continued interest: Patrick Jackson, Adam Fremantle, Richard Fremantle, Christine Sapieha-Fremantle, Philip and Katy Scott Coombes. A special thank you also to my cousin Nicholas Meinertzhagen, whose help and encouragement I have greatly missed since his recent untimely death.

For their help with this book, my thanks to: David Ainsworth, Richard Clark of Capital Punishment UK, Meredith Davies, Simon Fletcher, Graham Gower, Julie Gregson, Sarah Miller, Jon Newman, Colin Thomas, Rupert Willoughby; and thank you to my cousin Sir Roland Jackson, Bt, CEO of the British Association for the Advancement of Science for his advice and information on DNA.

For their help and assistance, my thanks to: The London Library, London Borough of Croydon Local Studies, London Borough of Lambeth Minet Archives, London Borough of Lewisham Local Studies, London Borough of Richmond Local Studies, London Borough of Southwark Local Studies, The Vauxhall Society, London Borough of Wandsworth Local History Department, Lavender Hill and Lewisham Cemeteries.

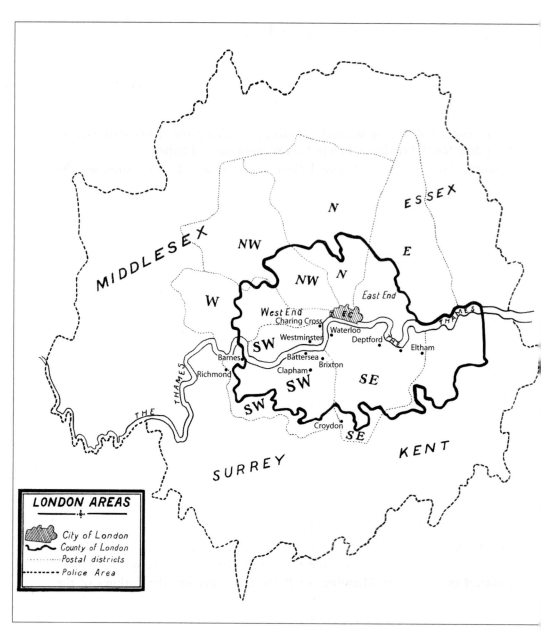

A map of the London areas covered by the Metropolitan Police Force, *c.* 1900.
(From L'Administration d'une Grande Ville – Londres *by Joseph E. Neve, published in 1901 by A. Huyshauwer & L. Scheerder, Gand.)*

INTRODUCTION

South London, that region of London derogatorily described by the crowd north of the River Thames as those parts 'South of the River', is home to a vast proportion of the working population of London. From as far east as Shooters Hill to the westerly confines of Richmond, from Battersea to Croydon, South London is rich in history, heritage and hubris.

South London has witnessed thousands of murders throughout the centuries, some of which have captured the public imagination for their very callousness and ferocity. Others have remained on the statute books as the foundation of some ground-breaking new laws and innovative new methods of detection. Many of these murders have shown not only the cold-bloodedness of the killers, but the raw hunger for sensation of the general public.

But what is it about South London that has attracted such a plethora of high-profile murders? Southwark and Bermondsey, for instance, were satellites of the city. Both fed the city from an early age and were incorporated into London early on. Yet both these areas remained, and do so to this day, largely working-class neighbourhoods that came to rely on the industrial era to ensure their livelihood. It was a fraternity of the London population that eked out its living by hook or by crook and attracted more affluent members of society to the area to indulge in their fantasies, their weaknesses and their passions – occasionally with fatal and criminal consequences. It was an area that encouraged its denizens to rise above the mass, sometimes in the only way they knew how – through crime, a sure and fast way to achieve a sense of importance. Once in a while the fast buck necessitated murder.

The earliest recorded South London murder was of an English Archbishop, Alphege, in Greenwich, in the eleventh century. It was a war crime made all the more heinous because the victim was a churchman. The murders of Christopher Marlowe and the Comte d'Antraigues were quite possibly political intrigue. The Mannings of Bermondsey became the darlings of the nascent press and the subjects of numerous novels, while the Brixton Baby Farming murder was the first of its kind to reach the courts and proved how low humanity could sink.

South London has a width and breadth of murders that quite literally take one's breath away. Two South London murders were connected to Jack the Ripper, owing largely to the over-active imagination of the press and the crowds, while another, the Lamson Case in Wimbledon, showed how even a member of a caring profession, a doctor, could be motivated to take a life, not save it.

Poison was the preferred method, although a good, hard whack did the trick just as well – except that it left rather a mess. The Bravo case in Balham was the apogee of the society scandal, in which poison and a good few suspects made and continue to make the headlines.

The twentieth century saw the rise of the South London gangs and the destruction of a good many homes owing to the First and Second World Wars. Some took advantage of the wars to dispose of unwanted people, as in the Baptist Church murder in Kennington; others took advantage of the wars' disruption by 'following the leader' and creating one of the most contentious cases in the history of crime, that of Craig and Bentley in 1952.

Murder is a waste of at least two lives, but what it can be is a catalyst for others to improve techniques in combating crime and in its detection, as in the first case where fingerprint evidence was used, in 1905 in Deptford, and in the use of DNA profiling during the past two decades. Fingerprinting, initially an intellectual game, was proved of lasting use in the Deptford murder in 1905 and since then it has remained an essential adjunct to the detection process.

Further advances in forensic detection have been made in the last fifty years – the two most important were to be psychological profiling and DNA profiling. DNA profiling is the latest, revelatory weapon in the fight against crime. This is covered in a separate chapter.

Peter de Loriol
2006

1

DEATH OF A SAINT

The killing of St Alphege, Greenwich, 1012

Tradition maintains that in the second half of the tenth century, more precisely in AD 953, Aelfleah, better known as Alphege, was born into a Somerset noble family. When in his teens he renounced the world, much against his widowed mother's wishes, and became a hermit in Deerhurst in Gloucestershire. His devotion soon attracted a following and his leadership got him preferment to a priory in Glastonbury.

The saintly Aelfleah soon tired of living in a community. He moved back to Bath where he served as an anchorite near the hot springs. Many of his disciples followed him. St Dunstan, primate of England, then convinced him to become the Abbot of a community of secular canons living nearby.

On the death of Aethelwold, Bishop of Winchester, in 984 St Dunstan had a vision that Aelfleah would be a perfect successor. He convinced the saintly personage to become the next Bishop. Here, in his twenty-two years as Bishop, he restored the church and organ, which, according to ancient sources, became another wonder of the world. Aelfleah was elected as primate of all England in 1006 and became the twenty-ninth Archbishop of Canterbury.

He was known and loved for his gentleness, his encyclopedic knowledge of the scriptures and his belief that conversion to Christianity should be done out of love and charity, particularly among the Norsemen. He attended the Council of Enham, and was the inspiration behind measures to be taken for national defence.

King Aethelred's reign was marked by an increasing presence of Viking invaders, eager to rape this industrious and fertile land. The ransom that Aethelred paid to stave off the invasions became known as the Danegeld. In AD 994 Olaf Tryggyeson, king of Norway, attacked London but was repulsed. He put the south coast to the sword. In a bid to stop the slaughter King Aethelred sent Aelfleah to parley with the Norwegian king. The result was that Olaf was confirmed as a Christian and was adopted as a son by Aethelred. In return Olaf promised he would never invade England again.

In 1007 a massive Danish fleet made a two-pronged attack on England. The first division was led by Earl Thorkell, the second by his brothers Heming and

Eglaf. They laid siege to and took Canterbury in 1011. Aelfleah, betrayed by Abbot Alfmar, was taken prisoner and brought to the Danish encampment in Greenwich.

In April 1012 the Witan (the Great Council) met in London and agreed to pay the Danes £84,000 in Danegeld to get them to leave. The Danes also demanded that a ransom of £3,000 be paid for the release of the Archbishop of Canterbury, their prisoner in Greenwich. Aelfleah refused to allow this further sum to be paid as he knew it would cripple the people of England even further. His Danish captors were so incensed that they drunkenly pelted the man of God with ox-bones and anything else on which they could lay their hands. Earl Thorkell tried to save him, but his men were out of control. On 19 April one of Aelfleah's Danish converts, Thrum, put the Archbishop out of his misery, killing him with an axe.

Aelfleah was murdered on the spot where the present parish church of St Alphege stands in Greenwich. His body lay there for several days until a miracle was reported. A Danish oar dipped into the worthy man's blood sprouted branches and grew blossom. The Danes relented and carried his body to London where the bishops Ednoth of Dorchester and Elfhun of London had him buried in St Paul's Cathedral.

St Alphege's parish church, Greenwich. (P.G. de Loriol)

The St Alphege window in St Alphege's parish church. *(P.G. de Loriol)*

Aelfleah was considered a martyr and pilgrims flocked to his tomb. In 1023 King Canute, the Danish King, was persuaded by his pious Queen, Emma, to have the remains of the Archbishop transported and reinterred underneath the north side of the high altar of Canterbury Cathedral. He was canonised in 1078. Both Archbishop Lanfranc and St Anselm agreed that sainthood had been achieved in the cause of divine justice. His last known words in answer to the Danes' demands of 'give us gold' were, 'the gold I give you is the word of God'.

2
DEATH AND DRAMA IN DEPTFORD

The murder of Christopher Marlowe, Deptford, 1593

Between Creek Road and the Thames, in Deptford, stands the church and graveyard of St Nicholas. Here, in the ancient graveyard, the body of the Elizabethan playwright Kit Marlowe was laid to rest in 1593.

This *enfant terrible* of the Elizabethan age, the 'Muses' darling', that 'pure Elementall wit', was the author of *Tamburlaine*, *Doctor Faustus* and 'The Passionate Shepherd'. He was idolised by Shakespeare, his contemporary, and later worshipped by Goethe, Swinburne and T.S. Eliot. He was a man of extremes: of wit, volatile temperament, candour, fashion, and passionate homosexual liaisons. He lived life and love in the fast lane and was killed at the early age of 29. His murderer is recorded in the church records: 'Christopher Marlow, slaine by Ffrancis Frezer, the 1. of June.'

This murder has caused controversy ever since. First, he was killed on 30 May; 1 June was the date of the inquest. Second, his murderer was not Ffrancis, but Ingram Frizer. Again, we are none the wiser. Was it really Ingram Frizer?

Let us look at the facts. William Danby, the coroner, and a jury of sixteen, viewed the body. The report, preserved in The National Archives, is remarkably detailed. It shows that Marlowe died from a fatal stabbing above the right eye and that the wound was 1in long and 2in deep. But what it doesn't say has led to centuries of debate: was it murder, accident, self-defence or premeditated conspiracy?

The problem with Marlowe is that the more one knows about him, the more confusion there is. What were the events that led up to his death? He was born in 1564 and studied at Corpus Christi

Christopher Marlowe, reputedly.
(P.G. de Loriol)

St Nicholas's church, Deptford, in 1790. *(P.G. de Loriol)*

College, Cambridge, where he received his BA degree in 1584. He may have fought in the Low Countries, he was certainly in Rheims during much of his university days, and he moved to London in 1587. Here he settled down as a playwright, mixing with the likes of Sir Philip Sidney and Sir Walter Raleigh, sharing a room with Thomas Kyd, and frequenting London taverns in bejewelled costumes with Robert Greene and Thomas Nashe. He was a complete extrovert, garrulous, quick-tempered, quite possibly an atheist, a maverick and cocky in more ways than one. It is therefore surprising to discover that he was employed by the government as a secret agent.

Shortly before his death the Queen, counselled that atheism was spreading, hurriedly ordered a hunt for heretics. Marlowe rashly pointed out what he thought were several inconsistencies in the Bible. This made him fall under the suspicion of heresy as 'all men in Cristianity ought to indevor that the mouth of so dangerous a member may be stopped'. Queen Elizabeth gave the order to prosecute him 'to the fule'. He had also written material that was deemed to be seditious, and it was highly unlikely that this unruly subject would remain free for much longer.

His room-mate, Thomas Kyd, was tortured into giving evidence against him, but before he could be brought before the Privy Council Marlowe was dead.

That 30 May 1593 Marlowe and 'friends' were relaxing, not at a tavern as previously thought, but at the house of Dame Eleanor Bull in Deptford Strand. Dame Eleanor was the mother of one of his classmates, Nathaniel Bull, and was a 'cousin' to Lord Burghley, Marlowe's master. His 'friends' were Ingram Frizer, a servant of Thomas Walsingham, Nicholas Skeres, an agent of the Cecils (patrons of Marlowe) and Robert Poley, also in the pay of the Cecils and lately in the service of Sir Francis Walsingham. These men were hardly friends of Marlowe's, but no doubt known to him.

Why meet for a 'feast' in the village of Deptford, right by the river? They drank from early morning until late evening. The coroner's report, only comparatively recently discovered, gives the official version:

'Four men met at ten o'clock in the morning in a room in the house of a widow . . . They passed the time in this room until dining, then spent a quiet afternoon together and walked in the garden until about six o'clock.' They then returned to the original room, had supper together. After supper, Marlowe lay down on a bed in the same room; while the other three remained at the table . . . an argument broke out between Marlowe and Frizer, concerning the payment of the 'recknynge' (the bill?). 'Malicious words were spoken whereupon Marlowe, "moved by anger", drew Frizer's own dagger, which was at his "back" and wounded Frizer twice on the head with it. The wounds were about two inches long and a quarter of an inch deep. Frizer feared for his life, but hemmed in by the others, was unable to

get away. He was able to struggle with Marlowe, however, and in that struggle Marlowe was stabbed by that same dagger. The wound was above the right eye, two inches deep, and one inch wide, and death was instantaneous.'

Ironically Ingram Frizer was never brought to book for the alleged murder.

The villages of the South Bank remained remarkably free of heinous crimes in the seventeenth century. The only bridge that connected the city to the South Bank was London Bridge, first built during the Roman occupation of Britain, then rebuilt in stone in 1176. Houses were erected on it. The bridge was removed in the late eighteenth century when two new bridges were constructed,

St Nicholas church, Deptford. *(P.G. de Loriol)*

Memorial to Christopher Marlowe, St Nicholas church, Deptford. *(P.G. de Loriol)*

one after the other, slightly upstream of the original. They connected the city to the great South Road to the Kent coast, through Southwark, and assisted in the city's march into the southern suburbs. South London had, however, remained largely untouched until the latter part of the eighteenth century, providing quiet residential villages, ideal for the city merchants who wanted to invest in estates near London – the perfect breeding ground for the highwayman!

3
STAND AND DELIVER

The murder of PC David Price, Southwark, 1795

Highwaymen were the muggers of the eighteenth century, although tradition maintains that their way of divesting people of their personal belongings was more chivalrous than those of their modern counterparts.

The truth was somewhat more prosaic. The highwayman normally started in his profession in his mid- to late teens, a bit like his modern equivalent. Some went on foot, but the more opportunistic ones, with an eye to staying alive a little longer, rode horses – ancestors of the bike? However, unlike his modern counterpart, the highwayman was usually caught and hanged by his early twenties – a short but cheerful life.

The 1790s, about the time Mr Abershaw started his reign of terror, saw an alarming resurgence of highwaymen. A typical example quoted from the *Gentleman's Magazine* of 1791 was:

> On Tuesday night, about ten o'clock, a Gentleman and Lady returning to town in a post-chaise, were stopped on Clapham Common, by a single highwayman who demanded the Gentleman's money, at the same time presenting a pistol. The lady being much frightened, he begged her not be any way alarmed, as he would not do them any harm. The Gentleman gave him a purse containing 20 pounds. The highwayman then wished them goodnight and galloped towards Mitcham.

The following account is of one of the more famous highwaymen of South London who ended his life at the 'three-legged stool on Kennington Common'. Jerry Abershaw was not a 'Gentleman of the Road'. By all accounts he was a tough villain. One innkeeper described him and his companion Dick Ferguson as 'terrible, cursing, swearing, and thrusting the muzzles of their pistols into people's mouths'. But he did have a sense of humour.

Jeremiah Abershaw, or Avershaw, was born in 1773 and started his working life as the driver of a post-chaise. By the age of seventeen he had dispensed with the low remuneration of the post-chaise for the more lucrative one of

Jeremiah Abershaw besieged. *(P.G. de Loriol)*

'Captain' of a small band of highwaymen who operated in all the South London commons and open spaces: Kennington, Clapham, Wimbledon, Putney and Kingston.

When in London he used to hide in a 'place in Clerkenwell near Saffron Hill, familiar to gentlemen of the road as the Old House in West Street, noted for its dark closets, trapdoors and sliding panels'. He also used the Green

Man inn at Putney Heath, but his headquarters was the Bald Faced Stag near Kingston, very close to Coombe Wood.

Mr Abershaw's success fuelled considerable efforts to try to bring him to book. He had said that he 'would murder the first who attempted to deliver him into the hands of justice'. Eventually word filtered through that he sometimes spent his ill-gotten gains at the sign of the Three Brewers in Southwark. A watch was kept on the public house, and this eventually paid off. Two Bow Street runners, David Price and Bernard Turner, finally found him there one cold morning in January 1795. As they stood in the doorway he cocked both his pistols and advised them to stand clear. They didn't. Two shots went off, one killing David Price instantly, the other wounding the landlord in the head. Jerry Abershaw was overwhelmed and taken prisoner.

He was tried at Croydon on 30 July 1795. His carriage took him over Kennington Common as they wended their way to Croydon. He stuck his head out and asked his escort whether they 'did not think that he should be twisted on that pretty spot by next Saturday?'

The presiding judge was Mr Baron Perrin; the counsel for the prosecution was a Mr Garrow. The trial was very short. Abershaw was accused of feloniously murdering a police constable in pursuit of his duty. He was also found guilty on a second indictment, of feloniously shooting at a Mr Barnaby Windsor. The jury pronounced the guilty verdict after barely three minutes.

The judge donned his black cap to pass the sentence of death; Jerry donned his and hitched up his trousers, asking 'with unparalleled insolence of expression and gesture if he was to be murdered by the evidence of one witness'. He was bound and transferred to a cell. There he reputedly amused himself by squeezing cherries and using their juice to draw pictures of some of his robberies.

His execution was billed for Saturday 3 August. Kennington Common was full. The whole of London wanted to see the show. He didn't let them down. He was trundled in a cart with another robber, Jack Ketch. His shirt was unbuttoned, he had a flower in his mouth and he chatted to all and sundry. Once on the gallows he didn't let his adoring public down. He kicked off his boots into the crowd 'to disprove an old saying of his mother's, that he was a bad lad, and would die in his shoes'.

His body was hung on a gibbet on Wimbledon Common overlooking the Portsmouth Road.

4

THE DULWICH LONER

The murder of Samuel Matthews, Dulwich, 1802

Dulwich had become the lordship of Edward Alleyne, the actor-manager, in the early seventeenth century. The lordship encompassed the whole village and what was to become Dulwich College. The woods, now almost completely disappeared, originally formed part of a huge forest that stretched from Shirley Hills, through the Norwoods, down to Wimbledon and Putney. They were largely the preserve of the Gypsy tribes that made up a large proportion of the population in this area.

On the morning of Tuesday 28 December 1802 a young man visited the lean-to in Dulwich woods that was the dwelling of a quiet, solitary, elderly man, Samuel Matthews. The 70-year-old's corpse lay across the entrance to his den, his jaw broken in two places, his pockets turned out and a hooked branch under his arm. It was obvious that the murderers had used the branch to hook the old man out of his lair and then despatched him.

An inquest was held at the French Horn pub in Dulwich. Samuel had worked in Cheapside, then moved to Dulwich, and on his wife's death had become a recluse, earning his keep as a jobbing gardener. Opposition to his setting up home in the woods had been fierce. His kindness and general humility won the day, however, and he was allowed to stay. Many dropped in to see him, including Gypsies.

The inquest's verdict of wilful murder engendered a public witch-hunt against the Gypsies, much the same as it would nowadays. Gypsies were considered thieves

Samuel Matthews, the Dulwich hermit. (*P.G. de Loriol*)

11

Views of Dulwich.
(P.G. de Loriol)

and robbers; they were beyond the pale and were only tolerated so long as they kept their distance. The Gypsies, though, were more than happy to share what they considered their kingdom with the Dulwich Hermit. It was more likely to have been two or more chancers who took advantage of what they considered a perfect victim, a lone, elderly man. Samuel was buried in the Dulwich cemetery chapel, and huge crowds sent him off.

5

A COUNT OF SOME ACCOUNT

The murder of the Comte d'Antraigues,
Barnes, 1812

Barnes appears fairly remote even now, but the Barnes of 1812 was a Surrey village that was one of the greatest producers of malted grains for the London and Surrey breweries. It was a quiet backwater with large houses and gardens for the gentry, and supported a population of about 900.

Barnes Terrace faced the river, as it does now. The road below it was part of the lower road that leads to Mortlake and Richmond. The bank had not been built up and the Thames water gently lapped the lower ground below the road. The quirky terraced houses, built in the middle of the eighteenth

Barnes Terrace, 1823. *(P.G. de Loriol)*

13

Antraigues House, Barnes Terrace.
(P.G. de Loriol)

century, fronting the Thames and Chiswick meadows, were the favourite summer retreat of Londoners. Number 27 was the home of the Comte and Comtesse d'Antraigues. It was to be a fatal summer for them both.

Emmanuel Henri Louis Alexandre de Launay, Comte d'Antraigues (1753–1812) was a tall, handsome, imperious and hot-headed Frenchman. He appeared, to all intents and purposes, to be one of the many émigrés who had sought the protection of the British government. The Comte d'Antraigues, however, was not part of that merry band of exiles. He was a cold, callous and merciless intriguer whose influence spanned Europe. His life had been blighted by a cruel and vindictive former Jesuit monk, who had been engaged to teach him in his teens.

This evil tutor was to have a profound effect on the impressionable young aristocrat. Detestation of the miseries that had been inflicted on this youngster was the catalyst, as d'Antraigues was later to admit, for a life filled with hatred and vengeance. A chance reading of one of Jean-Jacques Rousseau's books, and a friendship with the great man, introduced this directionless young fellow to the concepts of 'Liberty', but without shedding any of his caste's prerogatives. His writings were to gain him notoriety and the dubious acknowledgement as one of the most famous reformist members of parliament in the dying days of the French monarchy, but his ideals didn't go as far as backing an elected government.

He had sought refuge in Switzerland when the Republicans took control of France, and machinated his way throughout Europe by setting up an information agency, or spy network. Working for the Spanish government, then German states, Poland, Sweden and Russia, he was feared, respected and vilified in turn by the Bonapartists, distrusted by the French émigrés, shunned by Saxony, disliked by the Russians and suspected by the English. Yet Napoleon's overwhelming defeat of the Austro-Russian armies at Austerlitz made it imperative for d'Antraigues to move to England. He applied to the Russian government (his current employer) for a posting and also for naturalisation papers.

His arrival in England in September 1806, caused a furore among the émigrés, a break with the Russians and alarm in the government. His

Comte d'Antraigues. *(P.G. de Loriol)*

deliberate misinterpretation of certain conversations with Russian authorities, carefully sent to the Foreign Secretary George Canning, were to warrant his becoming a protégé of the Foreign Secretary, a salary and naturalisation papers being rushed through. He was asked to remain in central London and to endeavour to keep well away from the émigré strongholds of Twickenham and Richmond. His arrival heralded a spate of burglaries at his different residences – all unsuccessful. His papers were too well hidden. He was regarded as a turncoat by his countrymen.

The comte and comtesse lived at their terraced home for four days a week. The comtesse, an ex-actress with the ego and shrewish temper of an actress manquée, and her husband, disillusioned with marriage and his nomadic existence, made a volatile couple. Her difficult personality meant that their servants never stayed with them for long. One, Friquet, he was sure was sent to spy on him. Frédéric Diderici, another, was treated and fed so badly by the shrewish comtesse that he left.

Finally one Lorenzo, a Piedmontese deserter from the imperial armies, recommended by General Dumouriez, was installed in April 1812. Ironically, the general had been in the service of d'Antraigues' greatest enemy, Napoleon. The comtesse treated the man as badly as she had his predecessors. He complained to no avail and proceeded to neglect his duties. The comtesse then rebuked the sensitive Lorenzo over an Italian dish he had cooked. She told her husband, who threatened him with deportation. A deserter's lot was an unhappy one and it seems that the volatile Piedmontese had had enough.

The events of the quiet, sunny summer morning of 22 July 1812 were recounted by *The Times*, the *Courier*, the *Examiner*, the *Morning Post*, the *St James's Chronicle* and the *Morning Chronicle* in the following days. But the events that took place seem to have been blurred.

The count had ordered a carriage for 8 a.m. He had an appointment with Canning at 10 a.m. The coach arrived five minutes early and Lorenzo placed a can of cooking oil inside, made to return to the house, but was stopped by Susannah Black, a maid, who asked him to open the carriage door for the emerging comtesse. He ignored the request and walked past her to go back into the house just as the count was descending the stairs laden with papers. A pistol shot rang out and a servant, Elizabeth Ashton, ran into the hall to see Lorenzo with a gun in one hand and a long dagger in the other. He plunged the dagger into the count's shoulder. Ashton fled to the White Hart public house shouting 'Murder!' The countess asked the coachman what the matter was and returned to the front door, where Lorenzo stabbed and shot her. The bloodied count tottered to the front door. The coachman, Hebditch, ran to the fatally stabbed countess. She told him it was Lorenzo. Ashton returned from the public house to see the countess lying on the pavement, and Susannah Black ran for help. Ashton helped the countess back into the parlour. The weakened count pursued Lorenzo up the stairs. A shot was heard, followed by another. The coachman ran upstairs to find a dead Lorenzo and a dying count by his bedside. A surgeon finally came, too late for both the count and his wife.

The next day an inquest was held at the White Hart before Charles Jemmet, the Coroner. The empanelled jury returned a verdict of wilful murder of the count and countess by Lorenzo, who had subsequently committed suicide, being of sound mind.

What was curious was that there was a disagreement about who had been attacked first. What was subsequently discovered was that Lorenzo was a close friend of a Corsican servant of the Duke of Cumberland. The Corsican was a Jacobin and had attempted to murder the duke, then committed suicide. Lorenzo had received a letter a few days beforehand. He had appeared distraught on reading it and had then burned it. Another assertion emerges from the *Dictionnaire de la Révolution*, stating that two Napoleonic agents had been sent to England to convince Lorenzo to kill his master. Whatever the circumstances, the reason for the murder was never made clear. The government acted swiftly and sequestered all the count's documents.

6

THE LAMBETH MURDER

The murder of Mrs Whinnett,
Lambeth, 1830

In 1830 Lambeth was fast becoming a southern suburb of London. The building of Blackfriars and Westminster Bridges had enabled people from the city to move south of the river in search of cheaper accommodation and heavy settlements had sprung up between Lambeth Palace and Vauxhall Gardens. The population of Lambeth was 18,000 in 1801 and by 1830 was well over 30,000. Princes Street was in this dense settlement, opposite what is now the Albert Embankment. The Princes Street of 1830 was a busy, affluent, mercantile road. Number 30 was a marine store dealer's run by a forceful widow of about 60 years of age, Mrs Jane Whinnett, also known as Mrs Witham.

Mrs Whinnett was a woman of means and, like many business people in Lambeth, kept two large dogs to protect the shop. She had had a numerous family, but only her youngest son, Samuel, and one of her married daughters, Mrs Norris, her husband George and their child lived on the premises. Mrs Whinnett also had a lodger, Thomas Witham, a barge-builder about 25 years younger than she, who it later transpired was her second husband.

The afternoon of 19 August 1830 was no different from any other. The extended family all had tea together at about 4.30, then Mr and Mrs Norris and child left for Camberwell Fair and Thomas Witham and Samuel went to work. Mrs Whinnett was left to wash up the dishes.

Thomas Witham returned home at about ten past seven to find the front door locked. His next door neighbour, Mrs Poyne, told him it was no use knocking as everybody had gone out. Thinking his good wife to be out, he went to a local pub, the Three Merry Boys, and came back at about nine to find the door still locked, and Samuel sitting on the doorstep. They both agreed to try to break into the house through a back window. Once inside, they lit a candle and found the bloodied body of Mrs Whinnett lying on the kitchen floor. She had been bludgeoned to death. Her head was a mess: one

The Universal Pamphleteer.

A CORRECT HISTORY

OF THE

Horrid & Mysterious

MURDER OF MRS. WHINNETT,

ALIAS WITHAM,

At Lambeth, on the 19th of August, 1830;

WITH

A FULL REPORT

OF

THE CORONER'S INQUEST,

Held on the 21st and 25th of August,

INCLUDING

THE VERDICT OF THE JURY, AND EVERY FACT THAT HAS TRANSPIRED
RELATIVE TO THE DREADFUL EVENT.

THE UNIVERSAL PAMPHLETEER,

Consisting of Scarce, Instructive, and Entertaining Tracts on all Subjects, comprises—
Lives of Remarkable Persons—Facts and Romances from History—Tales and Legends
—Extraordinary Trials, Adventures, Phenomena, and Crimes—Abstracts of Acts of
Parliament—Arts and Treatises, &c. &c.
Each Pamphlet contains eight closely-printed octavo pages; and the Work is embellished
with superior illustrative Embellishments on Wood.

The coroner's inquest into the murder of Mrs Whinnett. *(P.G. de Loriol)* eye dangled out of its socket, the nose was a bloodied mass of cartilage and brains protruded from her scalp. The floor was awash with her blood and a bloodied coat, belonging to one of her sons, was laid across her legs. The neighbours were advised and a search was made of the house to see whether anything was missing. Nothing was. What was even stranger was that the dogs had never once barked. The Lambeth Association offered a reward and constables made a fruitless search for the perpetrator of this foul deed.

The Surrey coroner, Mr Carttar, convened an inquest on Saturday 21 August. Thomas was the first to give evidence. He originally said that he had been at the pub for half an hour, but later admitted to it being nearer 9.30 when he returned home. He had asked Samuel if his mother was home and was told that she and the others had gone to Camberwell Fair. He thought this strange, and that there was something the matter. He had knocked on his neighbour's door and gone through their garden to the back window, letting Samuel in through the front door. They had found the corpse in the back room and called the police. He then admitted to the court that he and the deceased had been married at St Anne's, Soho.

George Norris was the next to give evidence. He was a hoop-shaper, married to the deceased's daughter and living on the premises with his wife and child. He had long harboured a suspicion that his mother-in-law and Thomas Witham had married about two years before. They seemed, however, to get on very well. He and his family had gone to Camberwell Fair and stayed until 10.30, when they had been told that his mother-in-law had been killed. They had come home immediately. He also told the court that his mother-in-law had made a will in favour of his wife and brother-in-law. His wife gave the same evidence.

A Mr Reeves, a neighbour, who had also been to the fair, witnessed George and his family there and had been the one to tell them of the murder. Meanwhile, a John Gough had been taken into custody on suspicion of the murder. The surgeons agreed that the blows had killed the victim, and two other neighbours had sworn that they had seen no one around the house all afternoon. One of them also added that Thomas Witham had a good reputation and was not a lady's man. Gough was brought in and, despite neighbours' idle gossip, proved that he had been nowhere near the house in the afternoon.

Some witnesses stated that the front door was shut before 4.30, others after. Other witnesses stated that the door was open at 6.30. Joseph Anthony, a co-worker of Thomas's, was adamant in his evidence that Thomas Witham had been working with him all the time that he had stated. The coroner then summed up and the jury returned a verdict of 'Wilful murder against some person or persons unknown'. Thomas Witham left the court a free man, determined to contest his wife's will.

If, as we know, the dogs did not bark, surely the killer must have been someone they knew and trusted. The finger of suspicion seems to fall fairly on young Thomas Witham.

7

THE PINE-APPLE TOLL GATE MURDER

The murder of Hannah Brown,
Lambeth, 1836

Financial gain, or greed, is one of the main reasons for murder. This case was a typical example. It was to be one of the most talked-about cases of the nineteenth century because of its gruesomeness. The perpetrator would have been on police files many years before the murder had the police been more organised. But this was the infancy of the police, when people could still get away with murder – but not in this case. Just how could a murder committed in the heart of Lambeth be concealed from the public long enough for the perpetrator to flee the country? The following case will show how, but the final twist will be left to Justice.

Mrs Hannah Davis was happy. She was married to Evan, who did well with his cabinet-making. He had provided her with a good home, 45 Bartholomew Close, Smithfield. She was looking forward to the wedding of her friend, Mrs Hannah Brown, at St Giles's-in-the-Fields the next day, 25 December 1836. Mrs Brown would then become Mrs James Greenacre. Mrs Davis's daughter was to be a bridesmaid, her husband was to give Mrs Brown away, and the happy couple were to dine with them the next day before departing for America and a new life – the Davises were cordially invited there, to Mr Greenacre's 1,000 acres . . .

Yes, Mrs Brown was not young: she'd been married twice before and was about 45, a strong, handsome woman, despite a torn left ear, who earned her living as a washerwoman in Union Street, by Middlesex Hospital. She'd put away a tidy sum, £400 so she said. Mrs Davis thought of the last five years since she had met her friend . . . It was late, gone 10 o'clock, and cold outside. Horrible, these winter months. Well, at least she had a good fire going.

The banging on the door woke Mrs Davis from her reverie. She cautiously opened the door. My, my! It was Mr Greenacre of Lambeth, her friend's intended! A nice man, with a good estate, a little older than Hannah Brown, well turned out, of average height, a heavy coat protecting him from the harsh weather. He had what looked like a bag under his arm. He looked agitated – no, more than that, very angry, barely containing himself.

Before she could say anything he asked whether she had seen her friend. No, not since her last visit some two weeks ago . . . He rushed with his explanation. He had looked into Mrs Brown's affairs and discovered that she had been deceiving him about her circumstances. He had had some words with Mrs Brown and eventually come to the conclusion that it was inadvisable for them to marry. It was cancelled. He bade her goodnight, and left quite abruptly. Upset, Mrs Davis went to tell Evan.

Mrs Glass, of Windmill Street, Tottenham Court Road, patiently waited for her friend Mrs Brown on that same night. Mrs Brown was due to stay with her for the night, before her nuptials the following day. She never arrived.

Mrs Blanchard was the owner of a broker's shop in Goodge Street, off Tottenham Court Road, a very good friend of Mrs Brown's and, as it happened, the landlady of a Mr Gay – the estranged brother of Mrs Brown – and his wife. Mrs Blanchard and Mr Gay had heard that the wedding was off and were slightly apprehensive that Mrs Brown hadn't visited them. She would probably come when she got over it.

The well-dressed gentleman who appeared at the door of Mrs Blanchard's shop on the evening of Tuesday 27 December introduced himself as the Mr Greenacre who was to have married Mrs Brown. He was asked in but refused, saying that he was in a hurry and just wanted to advise her that Mrs Brown had 'grossly imposed on him' and had tried to purchase goods in a tally-shop in his name. He added that he had discovered she had no property and that their marriage would have plunged both into misery. Mr Gay appeared on the scene and was introduced as Mrs Brown's brother. At this, Mr Greenacre cut the conversation short, bade them 'good evening', and hurried away.

Mrs Brown's absence started to worry her friends and acquaintances. They asked around, but no one knew anything.

London was appalled by the story that emerged in the ensuing days. A labourer was walking to work on 28 December, on the newly developed Pine-Apple Gate, off Edgware Road. He saw a bloodied sack leaning against a wall and opened it . . . to find a human torso. He ran to find a policeman. The body was carted to Paddington police station and an inquest was held at the White Lion Inn, Edgware Road. A verdict was returned of 'wilful murder against some person or persons unknown'.

Noting that there were some wood shavings and some rags in the bag, the police made various enquiries, but there was nothing to go on.

On Friday 6 January 1837 a bargeman, 'Berkham Bob' Tomlin, found the Ben Johnson lock gates of the Regent's Canal, near Stepney, hard to operate. The lock-keeper used a long, hooked pole to dislodge the obstruction. It was a human head. The jawbone was broken, one of the eyes was missing and an ear was slit. Mr Girdwood, the Paddington district surgeon, examined the torso and head and declared that the head and trunk were part of the same body. During the next few days the papers sold out, and the head was duly deposited, preserved in spirits, at Paddington police station.

On Thursday 2 February a young man was cutting osiers in Mr Tenpenney's field, near Cold-Harbour Lane, Brixton, where the railway line now runs between Shakespeare Road and Hinton Road, when he came across an old sack on the ground. He opened it to find the remains of human thighs and legs. The police carted the grisly remains back to Paddington police station, convinced that the legs belonged to the rest of the body. There were, curiously, some wood shavings at the bottom of the bag.

Mrs Gay was convinced that the remains belonged to her sister-in-law. She finally persuaded her husband to go and view the head. He did, and recognised his sister immediately. Her other friends also viewed the head and confirmed that the remains belonged to Mrs Brown.

The police took the details. She had last been seen on Christmas Eve, quitting her rooms at Union Street to accompany her intended to his house. It was obvious that the only person who could possibly account for her last actions was her fiancé, James Greenacre of Lambeth. A police officer, Inspector Feltham, was put in charge of the investigation and a warrant for the arrest of James Greenacre, dated 26 March, was issued. It took a little while for Feltham to find Greenacre's address, 1 St Albans Place, Lambeth.

Feltham and another policeman duly presented themselves at the house. Mr Greenacre initially told them he knew of no Mrs Hannah Brown, and then conceded that he was to have married a Mrs Brown, and had they arrived the next day they would not have found him as he would have sailed for America. The packed trunks in his rooms seemed to prove this. The younger woman sharing his bed attempted to conceal something in her hands. Feltham commanded her to give him what she had hidden: a watch, two rings and a pair of earrings. Miss Sarah Gale was then asked to dress, and they were both placed under arrest. She collected her child from the adjoining room and they and the packed trunks were taken to Paddington police station.

Upon minute inspection, some of the clothes in the trunks seemed to be very similar to the rags found in one of the sacks, and some of the articles seemed to belong to the dead woman.

The desperate detainee tried to hang himself in his cell but was revived by a surgeon. The suspects were then taken in a coach to the magistrates' court on Marylebone High Street.

Gradually Mr Greenacre's life was unfolded. He had been born in Norfolk, but had established himself as a grocer in Southwark. He was appointed an overseer of the parish of St George and had married the daughter of the landlord of the Crown and Anchor tavern in Woolwich, a Miss Ware. His wife died of a fever and he contracted a second marriage with a Miss

Romford. He had seven children by his second marriage, five of whom died, as well as their mother. His third marriage was to a propertied widow, the daughter of a Mr Simmons of Bermondsey. His business had prospered and his third wife's dowry brought him a dozen properties on Bowyer's Lane (now Wyndham Road) and Windmill Lane (today's eastern end of Bethwin Road), between Camberwell Road and Camberwell New Road.

Unfortunately his good fortune ended when he dabbled in untaxed and spurious tea. The Board of Excise fined him heavily. He had two options: bankruptcy and prison in England, or emigration to America. He chose the latter, easier on the purse and on the health. He left his wife, but took his youngest boy. While he was in America his wife died. He married again, to a 19-year-old woman of means, and then left his new wife and his young son to fend for themselves while he travelled back to England. Here he lived in one of the few houses he had managed to keep from his creditors, 6 Carpenter's Place, Walworth Road, and plied his trade as a cabinet-maker. It was here that he met Sarah Gale and her daughter. She became his mistress and bore him a child. Neighbours thought of her as Mrs Greenacre. Her dependence on him

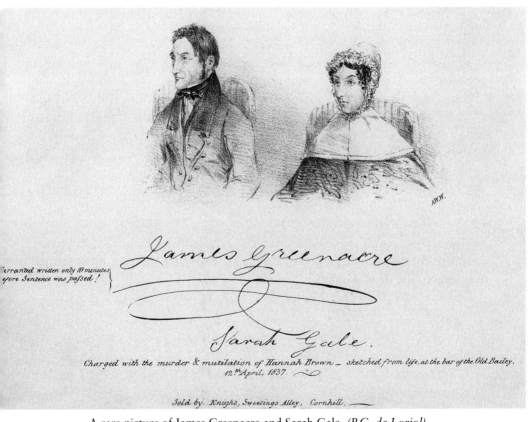

A rare picture of James Greenacre and Sarah Gale. (*P.G. de Loriol*)

became apparent when he convinced her to get rid of her child. Meanwhile he had met a Mr Ward, cabinet-maker in Tottenham Road. Mr Ward introduced him to Mrs Hannah Brown, a woman of property.

At the hearing Greenacre admitted that he had given Sarah Gale notice to quit before Hannah Brown's arrival. Hannah Brown arrived on Christmas Eve with her boxes, and a little worse for wear. They had a quarrel, and in a fit of pique he pushed her chair back. She hit her head against some wood. He tried to revive her, but she was dead. He panicked and chopped her up, distributing her body in various parts of the capital. He also said that Miss Gale played no part in this.

The crowds bayed at Greenacre and Gale on their return to jail. They were re-examined the following Saturday and arraigned at the Old Bailey on 10 April for the wilful murder of Hannah Brown, Miss Gale being an accessory. The judges were Lord Chief Justice Tindal, Mr Justice Coleridge and Mr Justice Coltman.

The sack, it turned out, was the property of Mr Ward. It contained wood shavings from his premises and linen cloth that matched exactly with a frock belonging to Gale, found on Greenacre's premises. It was also established that two pawn tickets found in the prisoner's pockets were for two silk gowns belonging to the deceased and that the trinkets taken from Miss Gale had belonged to Mrs Brown. The surgeons determined that Mrs Brown had been dealt a blow to the head which had dislodged an eye and that she had been cut up while still alive, the saw being found in the prisoner's tool box. The prisoner remained calm throughout.

It was also established that Mrs Brown had been a fortune hunter who had tried to use Greenacre's name to obtain credit. This serial polygamist had found her out and murdered her in his house, disposing of her body as he thought fit.

The 'guilty' verdict was returned after only fifteen minutes. Greenacre was condemned to death and, owing to his insistence that Gale had nothing to do with the murder, she was sentenced to penal servitude abroad for the rest of her natural life. The crowd gave a resounding 'hurrah!' Greenacre was hanged at Newgate on 2 May 1837. His last letter to his children warned them not to fall into sin and not to panic when present at fatal accidents. He reminded them that this seemed to be endemic in his family, as their Uncle Samuel 'killed your grandmother and shot off your Aunt Mary's hand'.

8
WHEN IRISH EYES ARE SMILING

The murder of Jane Good, Putney, 1842

The following case demonstrates how inefficient communication was before the telephone. Indeed, it was largely owing to this case that the Metropolitan Police force set up a detective branch in August 1842.

On the evening of 11 April 1842 PC William Gardner was called to Collingbourne's pawnbroker's shop on Wandsworth High Street. Collingbourne had just received a visitor, a 50-year-old Irish coachman, Daniel Good, working at Granard Lodge – one of the large houses on Putney Park Lane (between Upper Richmond Road and Putney Heath).

Daniel Good had bought a pair of trousers 'on tick' and stolen another. Samuel Dagnell, the shop assistant, had noticed the theft. PC Gardner, accompanied by Dagnell (to identify the suspect) and a young man called Speed (to identify Granard Lodge), trudged across the darkening heath to Good's employers.

The head gardener, Thomas Oughton, brushed Good's objections aside and told the party they could search the premises. Two of the four stables were searched, but to no avail. At the third stable Good remonstrated, but he was forced inside with the searchers. PC Gardner had uncovered Good's hiding place – 'Here's a goose!' he cried. Good rushed out, locking the stable doors behind him. The trapped men found themselves looking at the disembowelled remains of a woman's torso. Speed tried to open the doors with a pitchfork. Eventually they forced their way out and raised the alarm. Meanwhile, Good had fled across Putney Bridge, throwing his coat to the toll-man, saying he would return for it. (He never came back, and the toll-man wore the coat until it fell apart.)

The police established that the body was that of Good's pregnant, live-in girlfriend, Jane Good, alias Jones, alias Sparks, his third 'wife'. He was shortly due to take up with yet another woman, Susan Butcher, the 16-year-old daughter of a Woolwich carpenter. Miss Butcher was already the proud owner of a couple of Jane's dresses.

Nine divisions of the police force were involved in the hunt for the suspect. The 'route papers' system, the communications system that involved neighbouring division officers meeting at specific points to exchange messages and instructions for other parts of London, was woefully inefficient. Good was always a good few hours ahead of his hunters. The situation was not helped by an archly critical press.

The police descended first on one of Good's sons, who lived at 10 South Street (eastern end of Blandford Street), off Manchester Square, W1. The suspect had, however, left a couple of hours earlier. His forceful first wife, Molly, was interviewed at her home in Flower and Dean Street (now Lolesworth Close), Spitalfields. The house only received a cursory search and it could well have been that Good was still there.

Two police officers, Inspector Nicholas Pearce and Sergeant Stephen Thornton, future detectives, were deputed to continue the search. Good, however, had disappeared. He holed up at a nephew's in Deptford for a couple of days, then went to Bromley. It was here that his hunters lost track of him.

Dressed in a new fustian suit, he moved to Tonbridge, Kent, and worked as a bricklayer's mate. Unfortunately for him one of his co-workers, Thomas Rose, an ex-policeman, recognised him and told the local police.

The police discovered that Jane Good's body had been dismembered and most of it had been burned in the harness-room grate at Granard Lodge on 3 April. Good had suggested that it was she who had cut her own throat in a fit of jealousy over Susan. He also said that someone else had dismembered and burned her.

The presiding judge at his trial, Lord Denman, rebuked him for the 'indulgence of your inclination for one woman after another'. He was publicly hanged at Newgate on 23 May 1842, and in the same year the following poem was written:

Daniel Good. (*P.G. de Loriol*)

Verses on Daniel Good

Of all the black deeds upon Murder's black list
Sure none is as barbarous and cruel as this.
Which in these few lines wrote you I'll unfold.
The recital's enough to turn your blood cold.

In the great town of London near Manchester Square
Jane Jones kept a mangle in South Street we hear.
A Gentleman's coachman oft visiting came,
A cold blooded monster, Dan Good was his name.

As a single man under her he made love
And in due course of time she pregnant did prove.
Then with false pretences he took her from home
To murder his victim and the babe in her womb.

To his master's stables in Putney Park Lane
They went, but she never returned again.
Prepare for your end the monster did cry,
Yes time it is come for this night you die.

Then with a sharp hatchet her head he did cleave,
She begged for mercy but none he would give.
Have mercy dear Daniel my wretched life spare,
For the sake of your child which you know I now bear.

No mercy, he cried, then repeated the blow,
Alive from this stable you never shall go.
Neither you nor your brat shall e'er trouble me more,
There lifeless his victim he struck to the floor.

And when she was dead, the sad deed to hide,
The limbs from her body he straight did divide.
Her bowels right open and dripping with gore,
The child from the womb the black monster he tore.

He made a large fire in the horses' room.
Her head, arms, and legs in the fire did commune.
But e'er his intentions were fulfilled quite,
This dark deed by providence was brought to light.

To a Pawn shop the coachman he did go one day,
A boy said that some trousers he did take away.
A policeman did follow unto Putney Lane
The coachman and trousers to bring back again.

When in searching the stable a body he spied
Without head, legs or arms and ripped open wide.
Then a cry of murder he quickly did raise
And the coachman was taken within a few days.

And when he was tried, most shocking to state,
The evidence proved what I now relate,
That Daniel Good murdered his victim Jones
Then cut up his victim and burnt all her bones.

He soon was found guilty and sentenced to die
The death of a murderer on a gallows most high.
The blood of the victim must not cry in vain
As we hope that his like we shall ne'er meet again.

The moral of this story is as plain as can be,
That a maid must not trust a man such as he.
If she likes a man she must set him a task
And finally accept him when he drops his mask.

The execution of Daniel Good. *(P.G. de Loriol)*

9
ALL THAT GLISTERS IS NOT GOLD

The murder of Patrick O'Connor,
Bermondsey, 1849

Whereas Daniel Good's crime was sufficiently bloody for the Victorian mindset to attract huge crowds to his execution, larger than James Greenacre's, the outcome of the following case proved to be the definitive execution of the Victorian age. It showed the weaknesses of the system and the supreme power of the press. So much so, that the press embodied everything it pretended to revile – glorification of murder, pandering to the people and an almost pathological need to glorify murderers, turning them into central characters in a play that ended with a real hanging – effectively, anything to sell broadsheets.

Maria (de) Roux (1821–49) was an attractive, raven-haired Swiss woman. She was a lady's maid to Lady Blantyre – an occupation that would give her a taste for luxury and a complete abhorrence of poverty.

Her trip across the Channel to join her mistress on the continent in 1846 was to have fateful consequences. It was on this journey that she met Patrick O'Connor. He was a heavy-drinking 50-year-old customs officer at London's docks, with a sideline as a loan shark. He also had money invested in foreign railway stock. There was no doubt that his apparent wealth attracted her. They were to embark on an affair.

Another admirer was the lugubrious and weaker Frederick Manning. He was the same age as Maria and a guard on the Great Western Railway. Each man was aware of the other. Manning, conscious of his rival's wealth, told Maria he was coming into some money.

Frederick Manning.
(G. de Loriol)

29

Whom should she marry, the wealthy, older, hard drinker or the malleable Manning with the promise of a fortune? She married Manning in St James, Piccadilly in 1847. They first managed a pub, the White Hart, in Taunton; then Manning was sacked for being implicated in the theft of £4,000 from trains. They returned to London, where O'Connor convinced them to take the tenancy of a pub in Shoreditch. Maria continued her affair with O'Connor and absconded with him. Manning pursued them, and effected an uneasy reconciliation.

Maria Manning. *(P.G. de Loriol)*

The Shoreditch business failed. Maria blamed O'Connor for this and was determined to get her money back from him. By 1849 the Mannings had moved to 3 Minerva (or Minver) Place, New Weston Street, Bermondsey, at the southern end of Weston Street, south of Long Lane. They lived there somewhat beyond their means, and so took in a lodger, a medical student called Massey. Meanwhile she visited O'Connor at his home in Greenwood Place, off Mile End Road, and cajoled the older man to come to visit them.

Manning took a sudden interest in medicine, questioning Massey about whether a person under the influence of narcotics could still sign cheques, the properties of quicklime and chloroform, and where the weakest point of the skull was. Massey's growing suspicions got him thrown out of the house.

Manning bought a crowbar and a quantity of quicklime at about the same time. Mrs Manning finally convinced the reticent O'Connor to visit cholera-ridden Bermondsey. He first came with a colleague on 8 August. His second visit, on 9 August 1849, was his last. He was persuaded to come on the pretext that the Mannings' lodger's sister was visiting and they needed other company.

On the pretext of cleaning himself up for the visitor, Maria told O'Connor that he could freshen up at the sink in the basement kitchen. She shot him in the back of the head with a pistol as he walked down the stairs. The bullet did not kill him, so Manning finished him off with a crowbar. They stripped him, bundled him into a grave pre-prepared with quicklime under the kitchen flagstones, sealed it, and cleaned the kitchen with the help of an orphaned match-seller the next day.

Both Mannings tried to cheat each other. Maria went to O'Connor's house and stole cash, gold watches and continental railway stock, while Manning went to a furniture dealer to sell all their property. When he returned Maria had hired a cab and left with all her luggage, deposited her trunks at London Bridge and gone to King's Cross and bought a ticket for Edinburgh. Frederick, meanwhile, had taken fright when two of O'Connor's colleagues came looking for their friend. He fled to Jersey.

O'Connor's colleagues reported his disappearance to the police. The police searched the house and noticed the newly cemented flagstones in the kitchen. They lifted them and discovered the body. Superintendent Haynes of Scotland Yard started a manhunt, discovered that Maria Manning had bought a ticket to Edinburgh, and telegraphed his Scottish counterparts (the telegraph had only been in existence in Britain for the last ten years) only to be told that she was already under arrest because she had tried to sell some of the railway stock to a stockbroker. The stockbroker had already been informed that some railway stock had been stolen in London, and was wary of her French accent and the possibility of being the victim of a fraud. Maria was returned to London, charged with murder and held in Horsemonger Lane Gaol.

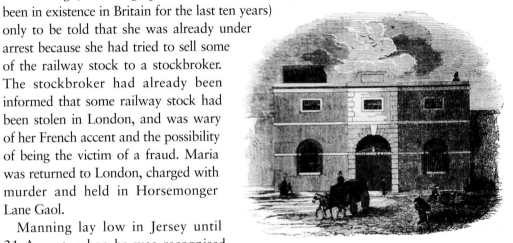

Horsemonger Lane Gaol. (*P.G. de Loriol*)

Manning lay low in Jersey until 21 August, when he was recognised. He was found asleep and arrested in a rented room in St Lawrence. Once in police hands, he told them that Maria had shot O'Connor and that 'I never liked him so I battered his head with a ripping chisel (crowbar)'. He too was returned to London and remanded to Horsemonger Lane Gaol.

The trial opened on 25 October 1849, before Chief Baron Pollock and Mr Justice Cresswell, the Attorney General prosecuting. Maria wore black bombazine (which, incidentally, put the material out of fashion for at least twenty years), maintained an icy calm and even took a hand in her own defence. She wanted to be tried separately to avoid Frederick's admission being used against her. Her counsel argued that, based on a statute of 1355, a foreigner was entitled to a jury of six Englishmen and six foreigners. This was denied because she had married an Englishman. She continued to fight, claiming that there was 'no justice and no right for a foreign subject in England'. Her husband did confess and both were sentenced to death, the execution being set for the morning of 13 November 1849. Maria threw bits of rue at the judge, a traditional practice of 'sweetening' the court with herbs.

Maria made a last-ditch appeal – very difficult for a defendant, as the Court of Criminal Appeal was not established until 1907. The appeal, which required the consent of the Attorney General, the Prosecutor, was, however, not granted.

The Central Criminal Court in the 1840s. *(P.G. de Loriol)*

The couple were hanged on the roof of the Gatehouse of Horsemonger Lane Gaol. A huge crowd assembled the night before, some saying that it reached 50,000. Charles Dickens paid 10 guineas to have a rooftop view, waiting up all night with a picnic hamper. The end was quick – too quick for Dickens. He complained that the hangman, William Calcraft, was 'unseemly brisk'. One wonders whether he, like the baying crowds, was as bloodthirsty as they. 'When two miserable creatures who attracted this ghastly sight were turned quivering into the air there was no more emotion, no more pity, no more thought that two immortal souls had gone to judgement . . .' John Forster (Dickens's biographer) was very impressed with Maria, writing,

> you should have seen this woman ascend the drop, blindfold, and with a black lace veil over her face – with a step as firm as if she had been walking to a feast . . . a close fitting black satin dress, spotless white collar . . . and gloves on her manicured hands . . . The wretch beside her was as a filthy shapeless scarecrow – she had lost nothing of her graceful aspect. This is heroine-worship.

Maria lived on as Hortense in Charles Dickens's *Bleak House*, and police wagons are named Black Marias after her. She was the last woman to be hanged in public. William Calcraft, however, continued his craft and performed the last public hanging on 26 May 1868.

10

WALWORTH MAYHEM

*The murders of Mary Wells Streeter and
Mary, Thomas and Charles Youngman, 1860*

Fresh-faced 27-year-old Mary Wells Streeter, daughter of a prosperous Wadhurst farmer, was excited at the prospect of seeing her sweetheart, William Godfrey Youngman, a tailor by trade, on Monday 30 July 1860. He would meet her at London Bridge station at eleven, take her to meet his family in Walworth and then take her to see a play in the evening. She could stay the night and go home the next day.

She had met William on one of her sallies into London. He was slightly younger than she, 25, but her father had found him an engaging fellow when he had come to visit them. He had persuaded her to take out a life insurance policy with the Argus Insurance company, but she would do anything for her intended. He had then asked her to destroy his letters before she came up – this she would not do.

William met Mary at the station and took her home, to 16 Manor Place, Newington (now SE17) to meet his mother, Mary Youngman. It was a three-

Houses opposite
Walworth police station
– similar to 16 Manor
Place. *(P.G. de Loriol)*

Walworth police station now stands on the site of 16 Manor Place. *(P.G. de Loriol)*

storey house. Mr James Bevan, the owner, occupied the ground floor, Mr and Mrs Philip Beard the first, and the Youngman family the second. It was a tight fit, the ceilings were thin and the staircase was communal, but they managed.

The two women went up to town for the day, and later, much later, William and Mary went to see a play. They returned home at around 11 o'clock, when Mary met the father, a tailor, and William's two younger brothers, Thomas, aged 11 and Charles, aged 6.

That night father and eldest son slept in the back room, while the women and the younger children slept in the front room.

Shortly after 5 o'clock on the morning of 31 July, Mr Beard was woken by his wife. She had heard some noise upstairs. They heard some running, a whimper, and then a dull thud. Mr Beard climbed the stairs to investigate, noticing some fresh spots of blood on his way up. As he reached the Youngmans' landing he saw Thomas lying in a pool of blood, his throat slit, and Mary Streeter lying a little beyond.

Beard rushed downstairs to Mr Bevan, shouting 'For God's sake come here – here is murder!' Both the landlord and Beard went back upstairs, Beard telling his wife on the way.

William, in a bloodied nightshirt, stood framed in a doorway, as if in shock. 'Mr Beard, for God's sake fetch a surgeon. I believe there is some alive yet. My mother has done all this – she murdered my two brothers and my sweetheart, and I, in self-defence, believe I have murdered her,' was all William could say.

Mr Bevan dressed, went out, and found a policeman, PC John Varney, of P Division. Varney accompanied Mr Bevan to the house, surveyed the scene, and told the young man to dress, noticing at the same time a bloodied knife on the floor and the body of the mother in the next room.

Youngman was taken to Lambeth Police Court and charged with murder. He was then tried on 16 August 1860 at the Central Criminal Court, the Old Bailey. Mr Justice Wilhams was the presiding judge, Mr Best the defence counsel.

Despite Best's fervent defence, it was established that the knife belonged to the accused, that his instructions to his sweetheart to destroy his letters seemed to show premeditation, and certainly that the life insurance policy warranted a more careful scrutiny. Youngman remained quiet throughout the trial, only repeating, when asked, that his mother had intended to kill him and he was only defending himself. But what really sealed his fate was that there was a suspicion that he had fully intended to kill his girlfriend for her life insurance and that there was a history of 'madness' in the family: both his paternal grandfather and paternal uncle had been in asylums, as had his maternal uncle.

The jury took twenty-five minutes to come to a decision. Youngman's execution was set for 4 September. He was led out in front of Horsemonger Lane Gaol to the scaffold. Some 30,000 people came to view. He thanked the prison chaplain for his 'great kindness. See my brother and take my love to him and all at home.' He greeted Calcraft, the hangman, with 'strap my legs tight and be sure to shake hands with me before I go'. Calcraft did just that.

Youngman might now have been remanded for psychiatric care, but justice then could not tolerate murder, however deluded the prisoner.

11

THE BRIXTON BABY FARMERS

The murder of John Walter Cowen,
Brixton, 1870

Increased social services and greater information and awareness about childcare in Britain have not reduced the number of babies born to single parents. Britain, it seems, leads Europe in pregnancies and births for single mothers, despite there being more than adequate measures in birth control. There is one economic factor that attracts some young single girls to have a child – the state has to house them. Nowadays it is incumbent on society to manage these families and ensure that the children are given a fighting chance.

Up till the early twentieth century this was not the case. A young girl who made the mistake of acceding to a man's wishes suffered ostracism. It was the death-knell of a girl's potential and future for her to have a child out of wedlock. Many would try to hide the fact. Either they would ensure that the child died in the first few months (which wasn't difficult up to the eighteenth century, as mortality rates were high) or the child would be put up for adoption.

The Industrial Revolution attracted people to the large cities in droves, seeking work. The Victorian era, known for its extremes despite the prudish façade, had a large working-class population in which more children were born out of wedlock than in any other social stratum. Improved sanitation ensured that many children survived. What could the young single mother do? For a long time the age of consent was 14. The young working girl could easily be swayed into having sex with an attractive buck, or even with an older man, for a few pennies – the consequences were disastrous. The following case highlights how certain unscrupulous individuals took advantage of the situation to feather their own nests and commited infanticide at the same time.

There were no employment opportunities for a young mother, or for a young woman who had illegitimate infants. Most young women did domestic work, factory work or embroidery. All these forms of employment kept them under the close scrutiny of their employers. The moment a pregnancy was discovered the woman would be fired. Once the child was born it was almost impossible for the young woman, with a bastard in tow, to find work. Pregnancy brought fear of starvation and deprivation for the child and its mother; alienation from their peers, family and society. The only recourse was to place the child in a workhouse, kill it, or 'sell' it to a baby farmer.

Baby farming, or professional adoption, filled a neat gap in the entrepreneurial market of the lower working classes. It was a mixture of adoption and childminding. It involved the payment of money either in weekly instalments or as a one-off by the parent to someone who offered to look after the infant, enabling the mother to return to work. In many cases there was an unspoken assumption that the minder would dispose of the infant in one way or another. The baby farmer's objective was to have as many infants under the age of two months as possible because it was more likely that the infants would die quickly, and their deaths would appear more natural. The dead child would be wrapped up in old newspaper and dumped in a street or into the river, avoiding burial fees. While a one-off fee of between £4 and £12 would provide the minder a good living, it was sometimes more profitable to adopt an older, more robust child for a weekly or monthly fee, enabling the minder to milk the client for as much money as possible, while gradually weakening the child until it died of apparently natural causes.

Baby farmer disposing of body. *(Police Gazette)*

Lambeth police noticed an upsurge in the number of infants' bodies, wrapped in newspaper or in cloth, found in the streets of Brixton and Peckham during the early part of 1870 – a total of sixteen. This forced them to appoint one Sergeant Relf to track down the source of the bodies.

A 17-year-old girl, Jeanette Cowen, gave birth to a little boy, John Walter Cowen, at a Mrs Castle's house on 14 May. Jeanette had been raped by the husband of a friend. Her father and his landlady, Mrs Guerra, came to collect the baby on 17 May, while Jeanette stayed on until the 28th.

Sgt Relf had been watching Mrs Castle's residence and noticed the young woman leaving, minus the baby. He followed her to Mrs Guerra's lodgings on Loughborough Road, Brixton, and talked to her father, Mr Cowen.

It transpired that Mr Cowen had answered an advertisement in the *Lloyd's Weekly Paper* of 1 May. This was an offer to adopt a child for £4. He had met a 'Mrs Willis' at Brixton railway station. Mrs Willis told him that she was childless and desperately wanted a child of her own.

The reality was somewhat more prosaic. Mrs Willis was an educated 35-year-old, the widowed Margaret Waters. Her husband's death had broken her comfortable lifestyle. She had tried her hand at various business ventures but had failed in all of them. She took in lodgers to make ends meet, and one of them, the mistress of a city gentleman, had become pregnant and paid Margaret to farm the baby out. This was the inspiration for her future profession. She was aided and abetted by her younger and more callous sister, Sarah Ellis.

Margaret Waters advertised extensively in the press as an adopter. She also re-farmed the babies for weekly payments and even rid herself of children by asking a youngster to look after them in the street and then clearing off.

Mr Cowen said that he had agreed to allow Mrs Willis to adopt the baby. He had handed it over at Walworth railway station. She had refused to give him her address as she did not want to have the child she had adopted taken from her – a canny move, as adoption had no legal status.

Mr Cowen had done this for his daughter's good, but he also cared about the fate of his little grandson. Mrs Willis came by a few days later to report on the infant's progress, as agreed. This time she refused to take any money from Cowen, let alone the stipulated fee.

Relf started to scan the *Lloyd's Weekly Paper* for adoption advertisements. On 5 June he noticed the following:

ADOPTION: A Good home, with a mother's love and care, is offered to a respectable person, wishing her child to be entirely adopted. Premium £5 which includes everything. Apply, by letter only to Mrs Oliver, Post Office, Goar Place, Brixton.

'Mr Martin' wrote an interested reply. He agreed to meet Mrs Oliver at Camberwell railway station on 10 June. Mr Cowen watched from a hidden spot but did not recognise the woman – because it was Sarah Ellis. He did, however, recognise the dress that had been worn by 'Mrs Willis'. Relf acted on this and tailed 'Mrs Oliver' to 4 Frederick Terrace, Gordon Grove, Camberwell. Gordon Grove, now Holland Road, is about ten minutes' walk from Loughborough Road.

The following morning Sgt Relf, accompanied by Mr Cowen and Mrs Guerra, forced an entry into 4 Frederick Terrace, surprising the two sisters. There they found five filthy, stinking, malnourished and drugged infants on a sofa – one of which was the baby Cowen. Four more were found in the backyard. Mrs Guerra barely recognised the baby Cowen. She said that 'there was barely a bit of flesh on the bones of Miss Cowen's child, and I could recognise it only by the hair. It did not cry at all, being much too weak for that, and it was evidently dying. It was scarcely human; I mean that it looked more like a monkey than a child. It was a shadow.'

The two sisters were taken to Lambeth police station and the baby was given to a wet-nurse. He died on 24 June. The sisters were charged with conspiracy to obtain money by fraud, and with the murder of baby Cowen. Their trial at the Old Bailey from 21 to 23 September drew extensive press coverage. The sisters denied murder and even proved that they had called a doctor for baby Cowen. They also stated that hand-rearing babies was fraught with medically proven dangers. The prosecution argued that the women benefited more from disposing of the babies by lump sum payments. Relf, on the other hand, discovered that the healthiest baby was a weekly payment case. The defendants' servant girl also testified that they sometimes left the house with a baby and returned without it.

The jury decided that Waters was guilty of murder and Ellis guilty of fraud. It was a contentious decision, as Ellis had admitted privately that she was the one who administered dope to the babies – dope she used to wean herself off alcohol. Waters, on the other hand, continually told the court that it was she who was the sinner and she who had directed her sister. Waters showed admirable courage in shielding her sister, although it was patently obvious that it was the sister who actively encouraged the early demise of their charges. Another point to consider was whether baby Cowen had died of narcotics poisoning or of disease, as he had died a full two weeks after his rescue.

Waters was hanged by William Calcraft at Horsemonger Lane Gaol on 11 October 1870. It was Calcraft's first private hanging. She was the first baby farmer to be executed and this was the first baby-farming case to have come before the courts.

The *South London Press* voiced its disgust: 'We shall witness in our midst the edifying spectacle of a woman strangled as a concession to one of those outbursts of public virtue which used to excite the derision of Macaulay and Thackeray, the latter of whom designated them "the safety valves of public vice".'

12

LOVERS' LANE MURDER

The murder of Jane Maria Clouson, Eltham, 1871

By the 1870s the population of London had passed the million mark. Twenty-two per cent of the working population was employed in the domestic field. Jane Maria Clouson, a pretty 17-year-old, was one such domestic servant. She had worked for nearly two years as a domestic for one Ebenezer Pook, a Greenwich printer of some repute.

Kidbrooke Lane ran from Blackheath to Well Hall in Eltham (now redeveloped as Rochester Way, SE3). It was a Lovers' Lane of the area. PC Donald Gunn had walked this beat twice already on the night of Tuesday

Kidbrooke Lane at the beginning of the twentieth century. *(P.G. de Loriol)*

The murder at Eltham, from an old print. *(P.G. de Loriol)*

24 April 1871. He was walking up the lane once more at 4 o'clock on Wednesday morning when he saw a woman on all fours, her head 'bobbing on the ground'. He asked what the matter was. She said nothing. He noticed that she was badly injured; in fact, one of her head wounds was so bad that he noticed some of her brain was leaking out. She looked as if she had been dragged, as her clothes were filthy. She pleaded for him to let her die. He made her comfortable and ran for assistance.

PC Gunn returned in a cab with Sergeant George Haynes. Haynes was later to testify that the woman was lying on her back and there was a pool of blood some 4ft away. She was taken to a local doctor, who in turn insisted that she be taken to Guy's Hospital, as her wounds were very dangerous. She fell out of and into consciousness, uttering some unintelligible words.

Haynes returned to the lane, where he found some widely spaced footprints that indicated a person running, and blood spots on either side of the Kidbrooke rivulet some 100yd up the lane, and he searched the nearby Morden College grounds. There he found a bloodied and hair-matted lathing hammer. This was eventually proved to have been the murder weapon.

Dr Harris at Guy's Hospital noticed several cutting wounds on the victim's face – two large wounds on the left side of her face and a third wound that had destroyed the right eye, breaking the bone around it. It was from this wound that the brain was protruding. The woman died at Guy's and the post-mortem examination showed that she was possibly some three months pregnant.

The police had a murder on their hands. They had by now worked out that the deceased had been in service. Her frock and hat were put on show at a local police station and by Sunday 30 April they knew who she was. A Deptford lighterman, William Trott, thought she was his niece as he and his family had been to her last known address, 12 Ashburnham Street, Greenwich, and she had disappeared a few days before. Her aunt also identified a mole on her left breast.

Jane Maria Clouson had only recently celebrated her seventeenth birthday. She was to marry a young man, one Edmund Walter Pook, a 20-year-old Greenwich printer (and son of Ebenezer). She had been summarily dismissed from her employment 'for being dirty' on 13 April, and had been befriended by a young woman and taken lodgings at Ashburnham Street, Greenwich. The police visited the lodgings and were told by her landlady, Mrs Hamilton, that Miss Clouson was to have met her 'Edmund' on the night of her murder.

Superintendent Griffin and Inspector Mulvany went to the Pook residence on Monday 1 May. Edmund Pook, an arrogant and confident young man, showed the clothes he had worn on the night. The police noticed his shirtsleeve was bloodstained – but he explained this by saying he had fits. Nevertheless, he was taken into custody and charged with murder before Mr Maude, the magistrate of Greenwich Police Court, on 2 May.

Edmund Pook, from an old print.
(P.G. de Loriol)

He was defended by a Henry Pook – no relation.

The inquest established that Miss Clouson had been struck between eight and ten hours before she was discovered. But how could the beat bobby have missed her? The Trotts confirmed that she had told them she was meeting Edmund at the top of Croom Hill on Monday evening. It was also established that Mrs Pook was behind the sacking – her eldest son had married beneath him and she would not abide a second mistake. A resident of Ashburnham Street also confirmed that Maria had received a letter which she had read, burned and then replied to. Another witness also stated that Maria had told her some three months earlier that she was pregnant. The police also discovered that a man answering to Pook's description had gone to a Deptford ironmonger, Mr Sparshott, to buy a hammer but had found it too expensive. Mr Sparshott had directed him to another ironmonger's. The second ironmonger had indeed sold a

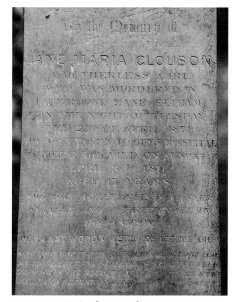

The memorial of Jane Maria Clouson, Brockley cemetery. *(P.G. de Loriol)*

hammer to an individual, but others in the shop had described him as a much older man.

Edmund said he was out on the night in question. He had gone to visit a lady in Lewisham. He had walked back, slipped in a gutter, and brushed down his muddied clothes at a friend's. He had also had supper at home and slept in the same bed as his elder brother. This was also confirmed. He had fits and on occasions streamed with blood – this may well have been the reason for the blood on his shirtsleeve.

The Times, Ebenezer Whitcher Pook's employer of some ten years earlier, constantly fed titbits by Henry Pook, allowed some useful gossip on the case to rule its pages. Young Pook was remanded in custody and the trial set for Wednesday 12 July, before Chief Justice Bovill, the Solicitor-General Sir John Coleridge prosecuting.

The case had angered many in the Greenwich area, because everyone could see who had committed the crime but none of the evidence against the defendant was provable. The crowds were kept away. The trial lasted four days. On the last day the judge, directing the jury, told them that the evidence was woolly, there had been no attempt to check Pook's alibi, and that they must disregard all the statements made by Jane before her death, as these were hearsay and therefore inadmissible. Accordingly, the jury acquitted Pook on 17 July 1871 – much to everyone's dismay.

Jane was buried in Lewisham cemetery. Her ghost was seen many times on Kidbrooke Lane, wearing a white dress and crying for help, its ashen face streaming with blood. The lane was avoided until the land was redeveloped.

13
OH SO SWEET

*The murder of Anne Watson,
Stockwell, 1871*

He was 'built like a bull'. With his head of thick grey hair, his sombre clothes highlighted by the faded white dog-collar around his neck, he sat impassively in the dock at the Central Criminal Court on 10 January 1872 as the case against him was announced by the prosecution, the Hon. G. Denman, QC. Mr John Selby Watson was a clergyman of the Established Church, aged about 67, and was charged with the wilful murder of his wife, Anne Watson, about 63 years of age, on 8 October 1871. He had been a schoolmaster and was a learned man.

The story of his life unfurled. Abandoned by his mother, John Selby Watson (1804–84) had been brought up by his paternal grandfather, a Dartford auctioneer. When his grandfather died he discovered he had been left £300, a brace of pistols and some books. Education was the tool for success. He enrolled at Trinity College, Dublin, studied Classics and became one of the Gold Medallists. He graduated in 1838. An educated but poor man, he decided that the cloth was the best means of advancement and was ordained as a priest by the Bishop of Bath and Wells in 1840.

He became a teacher and his efforts were finally rewarded when he was appointed Headmaster of Stockwell Grammar School in 1844. The next year, in St Mark's, Dublin, he married Anne Armstrong, a woman some three years younger than he who claimed that she had fallen on hard times, having previously lived in some splendour in a grand house in Dublin, but now living in a two-roomed apartment with her simple sister. While she undoubtedly felt something for him, it was fairly obvious that a woman of her age considered herself lucky to marry at all, let alone to a man who might be able to rescue her from a life that would otherwise have been spent in penury.

The married couple settled in the schoolhouse; his £300-a-year salary, although meagre, provided for them a style of life that made her relatively happy. As a result of his reputation and the growing number of students at the school, Watson's basic salary was increased, between 1863 and 1869, to £400. He added to his income by contributing articles to magazines and writing for Bohn's Classical Library, translating Roman and Greek authors

Houses further down St Martin's Road, identical to No. 28. *(P.G. de Loriol)*

and writing biographies on George Fox, Richard Porson, William Wallace and Bishop Warburton – the last being his most successful.

Mrs Watson's wish to live in a house of their own made him move to 28 St Martin's Road, a short walk from the school, a roomy house rented yearly. Having no children, a husband who read and wrote most of the time, and an income that was sufficient but below her expectations, made Anne Watson become shrewish. She took to the bottle and ranted against the servants and sometimes against her husband.

He contented himself with the knowledge that during his tenure as Headmaster the school had thrived, producing several students who had gone on to university. He was also universally admired by the students, for he was one of the few masters of the age who did not believe in corporal punishment, preferring to try to encourage students to do better rather than to chastise them. Conscious of his own bad start in life, he was also very charitable towards others in more straitened circumstances. He was respected and seemed to inspire confidence. This large, quiet man was a gentle giant.

The bombshell came on 30 September 1870. The school and its governors had presented him with a silver salver at the school assembly. The president of the Board of Governors had waxed lyrical about the school's attainments during the Headmaster's twenty-two-year tenure, had complimented him on his fair and inspiring headship – and then the letter came. He was asked to vacate his position at the end of term.

Watson showed the letter to anybody who cared to see it. He tried to reason with the governors, but to no avail. His secure lifestyle dissolved. His wife ranted. He locked himself in the study. He also cut down on his house servants, only keeping on two, one of whom, Ellen Pyne, seemed to be the butt of Mrs Watson's tirades when the doctor was out – as he invariably was, when not in his study. Watson tried to convince his wife that they needed to move to smaller premises, but she would have none of it.

The crunch came on 8 October 1871. Mrs Watson was drunk and took it out on him yet again. Goaded to an extreme, he beat her with the butt of one of the pistols in the study annex. He then tried, three days later, to commit suicide with prussic acid, but the devoted Ellen Pyne found him and called for a doctor. It was then that the dead woman's body was found. The police were called and Dr Watson was taken to Horsemonger Lane Gaol.

Dr John Selby Watson pleaded not guilty. The *Daily Telegraph* saw fit to sermonise on the difference between a murder done by a low-life and one done by an educated man, and on the conditions that push either to commit such a crime. Charles Turner, a trunk manufacturer of Clapham Road and a witness at the trial, confirmed that the prisoner had been interested in a trunk but had been unsure whether to commission it. The prosecution claimed that this showed intent that the prisoner wanted to hide the body. The defence said it was for his books and papers.

Modern flats now stand on the site of 28 St Martin's Road. *(P.G. de Loriol)*

Dr Watson killing his wife. *(P.G. de Loriol)*

Various doctors were called to the stand. None of them was willing to say whether Watson could be declared insane. But they did admit that he might have been suffering from 'melancholia' – despondency at his predicament. What did emerge was that Mrs Watson had been of a 'rather hasty temperament' – difficult and quarrelsome.

The presiding judge, Mr Justice Byles, summed up on the third day. Had the prisoner acted in a manner that showed he was in full possession of his faculties when he committed the crime? The jury took one and a half hours. Their verdict was murder, but they asked for clemency in view of the defendant's age and previous good character. The judge ordered that he be hanged. The *Globe* pointed out on 26 January 1872 that it was curious how so much effort was being made to commute his punishment to a life sentence because he was of previously good character, and that he was a man of the cloth.

His sentence was commuted to life imprisonment at Parkhurst Prison on the Isle of Wight. He remained quiet to the end and died of a fall from his hammock on 6 July 1884.

14

THE MADNESS OF
DR MINOR

The murder of George Merrett,
Lambeth, 1872

The Victorian dictum that 'only the lower and criminal classes habitually rise before 7 a.m.' certainly applied to the 34-year-old George Merrett of 24 Cornwall Cottages, Cornwall Road, Lambeth (now completely redeveloped as the South Bank Development, SE1). He was the father of a brood of six, with another on the way, and a stoker at the Red Lion Brewery, earning a weekly pittance of 24s.

The night of Saturday 17 February 1872 was a cold one. George Merrett left his home at 2 a.m. to walk to work. He walked down Belvedere Road towards Tenison Street and circled round the brewery walls. Angry, piercing shouts broke the silence of the cold night. A man ran towards him, gun in hand, and a bullet whizzed past him. He turned to run, but two more bullets tore into his neck. He collapsed against the wall of the brewery.

Police Constable 236L, on duty on Belvedere Road, heard the gunfire and rushed towards the noise. He ran across to a lone figure on the opposite side of the street and asked the man if he knew who had fired. The man replied that he had fired at a man because he 'should not be such a coward as to shoot at a woman'. The policeman arrested the man, took the revolver from him, and started to walk him back to the Tower Street police station. He met another policeman on the way and told him to check out Tenison Street. He did, and found George Merrett in a pool of blood.

The dying man was taken to St Thomas's Hospital, where he died on arrival. The American, for that was what he turned out to be, was initially questioned. He said he was Dr William Chester Minor, aged 37, gave his address, and said he believed that the murdered man was one of the Irish militants who attacked him nightly through his ceiling and from under his bed.

Sergeant Steggles, acting inspector at Tower Street police station, went to the prisoner's lodgings to check on his claims. He found a large amount of cash, gun cartridges, a US surgeon's diploma and a captain's commission dated 1867, as well as a letter of introduction and several unfinished watercolours. The gentleman was no ordinary criminal! Despite the American vice-consul's being present on Monday, Dr Minor refused his assistance.

But who was this obviously deranged American gentleman? Born in Ceylon (now Sri Lanka) in 1834 to American missionary parents, William Chester Minor showed an early aptitude for languages, reading and music. He learned the flute and, probably as a result of the austere religious teachings of his parents, showed an advanced interest in the nubile Ceylonese girls. It was decided, as much for his moral upbringing as for his educational benefit, that he be sent, at the age of 14, to an uncle in Connecticut. He did well, graduated from Yale University with a degree in comparative anatomy and then joined the Union Army as an assistant surgeon at the height of the Civil War. One of his duties was to brand Irish immigrant deserters with the letter 'D' – a duty he found sickening, affecting his somewhat unstable personality. He began to have paranoid delusions that the Irishmen would eventually seek him out and exact vengeance. His hard work earned him a captain's commission.

He was posted to New York after the Civil War. Here the repressed and progressively deluded man indulged in the pleasures of the fleshpots of the city. But his paranoia increased and the army transferred him to a lunatic asylum in 1868. He showed no real improvement, and was allowed to resign his commission and take retirement pay.

Profoundly troubled, he sought more carnal pleasures and came to London in 1871, settling in lodgings in one of the largest red-light districts, Lambeth. Here he indulged in his predilection for prostitutes and medicated himself after contracting sexually transmitted diseases.

His trial took place at Kingston Assizes Court in April 1872. The jury heard of his mental illness and noted that at the time of the murder he was not in control. He was found 'Not guilty by reason of insanity' and was certified a 'Criminal Lunatic' on 6 April and sent to the newly built Broadmoor criminal lunatic asylum, to be detained at Her Majesty's pleasure. His pension afforded him comfortable lodgings. He would be its longest resident.

An honourable man, he wrote to the widowed Mrs Merrett, apologising for the hurt he had caused. He also sent her money. She, in turn, accepted his apology and even visited him.

Dr W.C. Minor. *(P.G. de Loriol)*

His love of books and reading provided him with an escape from the reality of his incarceration and provided him with an impetus. An advertisement in one of the books given to him by Mrs Merrett, asking for volunteers to assist in the compilation of the *New Oxford English Dictionary*, prompted him to volunteer. He became one of the most important contributors to the dictionary and a great friend of its editor, James Murray. Minor's condition grew worse – he even tried to cut off his penis in remorse. Eventually, with Murray's help, he was repatriated to America in 1910 and was diagnosed as being schizophrenic. He died in 1920, largely forgotten until recently. Events tend to alter one's life, but it is extraordinary how a fatal event created one of the English language's great sages.

15

THE BALHAM TRAGEDY

*The murder of Charles Bravo,
Balham, 1874*

We find that Charles Delauney Turner Bravo did not commit suicide; that he did not meet his death by misadventure; that he was wilfully murdered by the administration of tartar emetic. But there is not sufficient evidence to fix the guilt upon any person or persons.

Such were the findings of the inquest held in July 1874 at the Bedford Hotel, Balham, SW12, into one of the most talked-about 'society' murders of the nineteenth century, and one of the great social scandals of the time, which demonstrated, warts and all, the obvious deterioration of a mismatched pairing.

The 19-year-old Florence Campbell, the favourite daughter of a rich Australian industrialist settled in England, had always managed to have her own way. When she met the dashing army officer Alexander Ricardo, her father acceded to her new demand – marriage. They were married on 21 September 1864. The doting father gave his daughter £1,000 a year.

By the spring of 1865 the marriage was in tatters. Florence had pressured Ricardo into leaving the army. He became bored, felt harassed and drank to forget, as well as picking up a mistress or two. Florence tried to pretend things were all right but his drunken, verbal abuse became too much. She fled to her parents in 1870. Her father remonstrated, she had a tantrum and her mother suggested that she go to Dr Gully's clinic in Malvern to recuperate.

The year 1870 was a seminal one for women. The Married Women's Property Act enabled women to retain earnings or property acquired after marriage. Dr James Gully was one of the celebrity doctors of the age. He was a small, dapper, balding man in his sixties. Saddled with a considerably older wife, he had made his reputation with his Hydro in Malvern. He was doctor to the rich and famous, and numbered Lord Aberdeen and Charles Darwin among his patients. He had also known the Campbell family since Florence was a child. Although not good-looking, he was immensely attractive to women – soon after she arrived, the young Florence realised that she was falling in love with him. Gully was a liberal and advocated greater freedom for women – something Florence could understand. At her instigation they became lovers. She made all the moves and dictated, as was her wont, when and where they made love.

In April 1871 Florence heard that her husband had died of chronic alcoholism. The fact that she was still his wife meant that she inherited his estate of £40,000. She was a rich woman. She convinced Gully to come with her to London. She lived in Barham House and he in Hillside – two large houses on Leigham Court Road in Streatham. She looked around for a property to suit her style and took the lease of a white-painted Gothic folly crowning Bedford Hill in Balham. The Priory was a magnificent mansion on the edge of Tooting Common. She hired staff to look after the daily running of the house, as well as a lady's companion, Jane Cox. Jane Cox was a small, bird-like woman, always immaculately dressed in black. The complete opposite of her mistress, she was quiet, orderly and a perfect mother-figure to Mrs Ricardo. The two became inseparable; neither could do without the other.

The Priory, Balham. *(P.G. de Loriol)*

In May 1872 the lovers were caught *in flagrante delicto* in a neighbour's house. The scandal among the prurient society of the chattering classes rocked the Campbells. They cut themselves off from their errant daughter. She then became pregnant and Gully performed the abortion – which effectively destroyed their affair. She was a social animal who could not live in purdah for the rest of her life. She had to find a new husband to make her respectable again. Enter 30-year-old aspiring barrister Charles Bravo, a typical product of the Victorian middle classes – a gentleman, a stickler for convention and a conservative dresser. He was also ruthless and lacked compassion for anyone outside his circle. Jane Cox had met him and thought him a good catch.

Florence was attracted by his zest for life, his passion and his wide interests. He was slim, of average height and good-looking to boot. By October 1875 he had proposed. Florence ended her now loose association with Dr Gully and told her fiancé about the affair. He in turn told her about his mistress and child in Maidenhead. He still wanted to marry Florence, but she began to think he was a gold-digger. This was confirmed, in a sense, when she invoked the right to keep her property and fortune after her marriage. He righteously countered by saying he would not contemplate not being master of his own house. They reached a compromise: she would give him the lease of the Priory and its furnishings and make a will in his favour. They married on 7 December 1875. She had regained her respectability; he had gained a rich bride.

Anonymous letters arrived for Bravo, accusing him of marrying for money. He thought Gully, who had remained in the neighbourhood, was responsible. One coachman was summarily dismissed by Bravo, much to his wife's chagrin. Then she became pregnant. Bravo assumed the mantle of the master of the house, dictating what the staff and his wife could and could not do, suggesting various ways of cutting back on costs. This didn't wash with his wife. She was too accustomed to doing things her way, especially now she was a rich woman in her own right. They fought like cat and dog. Their relationship went further downhill when she discovered that she could not dictate when they had sex. He resorted to a fairly common practice in the nineteenth century – anal intercourse. This was practised when couples did not use contraception – and most did not. Florence fled to her parents.

After much cajoling, she returned to the Priory. Four days later she had a miscarriage. This shattered Florence's constitution, let alone the damage to her psyche. She started drinking and asked her husband to sleep in the front room while the ever-present Mrs Cox ministered to her. Bravo hated and envied Mrs Cox.

In March Charles told his wife that he wanted to come back to her bed. She was deeply unsettled. The miscarriage had shaken her. She wasn't sure that she could have a child – the septicaemia that had followed her earlier abortion might have damaged her uterus. Bravo moved back into their bedroom and within a couple of weeks Florence was pregnant, to the discomfort of her

Portraits of the various figures in The Balham Tragedy. *(P.G. de Loriol,* Penny Illustrated)

parents. Then Charles was struck down with some strange vomiting sickness that lasted a day.

Spring was in the air and the house buzzed with constant guests. Florence miscarried again shortly into her second pregnancy. She was debilitated and once again banned her husband from her room. Her physician, Dr Harrison, was worried. Mrs Cox repeated her ministrations, including the obligatory alcohol.

On Tuesday 18 April the couple went into town. Florence left her husband after a morning's shopping and returned home. Charles returned home later and took one of the horses for exercise. He returned an hour later, shaking and sweating. He was helped off his horse and sat miserably in a chair until he decided to have a bath. He could not stand so the servants helped him upstairs. He felt well enough, though, to have supper with his wife at 7.15. It was disastrous. She drank too much and he shouted. Both went angrily to their respective rooms, Florence armed with a brandy.

At about 9 o'clock Charles staggered out of his room, shouting for hot water. Mrs Cox dashed into his room to find him vomiting out of the window. He collapsed and, helped by a maid, Mrs Cox put him in bed. They poured a bit of mustard water down his throat. He vomited again. Florence took charge and ordered the nearest doctor to be called, Dr Moore of Balham. Dr Harrison had already been called but he was further away.

Dr Moore told Harrison that Bravo was mortally ill – he thought he had drunk some sort of poison. Bravo's functions seemed to be shutting down. He had soiled the bed; the bed was bloodied as a result. Mrs Cox said he had been drinking Burgundy. Dr Harrison formed the opinion that Mr Bravo had ingested something such as arsenic. The two doctors searched the room for anything that might resemble it, but to no avail. Florence called for Dr Royes Bell and Dr George Johnson, the former a cousin of her husband and the latter vice-president of the Royal College of Physicians.

Charles came round shortly after the arrival of the latter two. He seemed fairly lucid. His cousin told him that he was dying. He took it stoically. Mrs Cox

An artist's sketch of the Bravo Inquiry at Balham, July 1876. (P.G. de Loriol, Penny Illustrated)

told Bell that Bravo had admitted to her that he had taken poison. Bravo was confronted, but admitted only to having taken some laudanum, something he took regularly. Bell became suspicious and searched Mrs Cox's bedroom, but found nothing. He then interviewed the staff. Charles's stepfather arrived.

By Thursday, Charles was slipping out of and into consciousness. Sir William Gull, Physician Extraordinary to the Queen and a close friend of Florence's father, was called for. He arrived and talked to Charles in a lucid moment – Charles maintained that he had only taken laudanum. Sir William left, sure that the poison was a much stronger one.

After making a will on Friday morning, Charles Bravo died at about 5.15 a.m. – some fifty-five hours since his first symptoms had appeared. He was 31. He was buried in South Norwood cemetery.

The inquest established that the death was murder, but no one could be prosecuted for lack of evidence. There was no shortage of possible suspects, however. Could it have been the devoted Dr Gully, anxious to get back to his paramour? He still kept in contact with Mrs Cox. Could it have been Mrs Cox, the devoted *éminence grise* of Florence? She was a perfect mother figure and totally selfless – or was she? She lived out the rest of her days in splendour in Jamaica, after inheriting a fortune.

Could it have been the wilful, artful and deceitful Florence? She was obviously frightened of having another miscarriage – which could lead to her death. She was also very scared of her husband's temper and tirades. Maybe she had had enough and made enough mistakes? She died only two years later, a lonely widow, by the seaside.

16
STARVED TO DEATH

*The murder of Harriet Staunton,
Penge, 1877*

Doctor Longrigg looked at the patient. She stank, her hair was covered in lice, her breathing was laboured, the pulse quick and weak. Her fingernails and hands were filthy, yet it seemed that Mrs Staunton was more than the middling sort.

Her body was so thin it made him wince. A woman of her build and height, 5ft 4ins, should weigh at least 8½st. This prone and emaciated shell of a woman was no more than 5st. She was dehydrated and hadn't long to live. He couldn't tell how old she was because of her state, but guessed she was in her late thirties. He could see that Mrs Patrick, who had fetched him on the recommendation of her landlady Mrs Chalklin, was rather inexperienced. He told her that he didn't think the unconscious woman would make it through the day – what an unlucky day, Friday the 13th! He prescribed absolute quiet and spoon-feeding beef tea and milk. She might rally. As he left, he promised he would send a nurse. He checked his fob watch – it was 10.20 a.m.

Ellen Gooding, the nurse, arrived about an hour later. The patient was unconscious. The doctor was fetched at noon, as the patient seemed to be slipping into a coma. Dr Longrigg

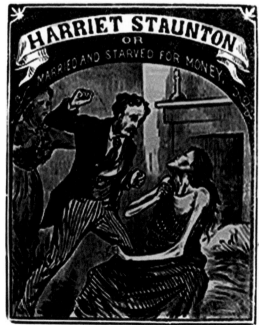

To be Continued in Weekly Penny Numbers
A Novel of Intense Interest, entitled

HARRIET STAUNTON
OR
MARRIED AND STARVED FOR MONEY.

No. 2 Presented with no. 1 in Coloured Wrapper.
PRICE ONE PENNY.
G. PURKESS, 286, STRAND, W.C.

The murder of Harriet Staunton. *(P.G. de Loriol)-*

only remained a few minutes. She died at half past one, attended by Mrs Gooding. Mr Louis Staunton – the woman's husband – and Mrs Patrick were in the next room. Dr Longrigg wrote out a certificate stating the cause of death – primarily cerebral disease, secondly apoplexy. He had not been able to make an examination as he had only seen the patient for a few minutes.

Harriet Staunton. *(P.G. de Loriol)*

His statement was based on what Louis Staunton had told him, and from his brief observations it seemed logical. Mrs Gooding tried to lay the body out, but the unbelievably filthy body was caked with what seemed like the bark of a tree. Mr Louis Staunton and another man said that they would arrange the funeral. It would take place the following Monday at Beckenham. They entrusted the flat keys to the nurse and left Penge.

Mr de Casabianca breezed a good evening to the postmaster as he entered the small post office in Forbes Road, Penge, on the evening of 13 April 1877. As he sorted his business a stranger walked in purposefully and engaged the postmaster in conversation. He could clearly hear what was being said. The stranger asked the post-master where he could register a death that had occurred that morning in Forbes Road. Was Forbes Road in Kent or Surrey? Half the road was in Kent and the other half was in Surrey . . . and the number would be? Ah 34, well then that was Kent . . . and was the lady from hereabouts? No, the dead lady was from Cudham in Kent.

Mr de Casabianca stood rooted to the spot. How extraordinary. His wife's sister, Mrs Louis Staunton was last heard of living in Cudham. Her family had good reason to think she was being kept there against her will and that she was being maltreated. Once the stranger had left he asked who the local doctor was and waited until the next morning to see Dr Longrigg.

The doctor had attended the deceased. He had signed a medical certificate. After hearing Mr de Casabianca's story he showed him the body. It was his sister-in-law. The doctor withdrew the certificate and ordered that the funeral be postponed and that the county coroner be advised. Mr de Casabianca then contacted the local police and told them his story. Sergeant Bateman went down to Cudham and arrested Mr and Mrs Patrick Staunton, Louis Staunton and Alice Rhodes on suspicion of murder.

The post-mortem was held at 34 Forbes Road on 19 April. Dr Longrigg and his partner Mr Pigott, Dr Bright, a friend of the deceased's family, Mr Wilkinson, police surgeon, a Mr Lister and Mr Harman, the latter on behalf of the accused, made a minute examination of the body. They decided that she had died of extreme and prolonged starvation. The coroner, after an inquest lasting from 10 to 19 May, then issued a statement that Mrs Louis Staunton had been wilfully murdered by the four held in police custody.

The trial started on 19 September 1877 at the Old Bailey. Sir Henry Hawkins presided. The prosecution was headed by Sir John Holker, QC and ably assisted by Sir Hardinge Giffard and Harry Poland. The defence team each represented one of the defendants. Montagu Williams and Edward Clarke headed the team. It had to be established whether Harriet Staunton had died through the 'culpable misconduct' of the prisoners, or even of one of them, and, if so, whether this amounted to murder or manslaughter. Would the eventual verdict of the jury decide whether some or all of the defendants were guilty of committing the deed or of abetting it?

The story unfolded. Harriet Staunton was one of the daughters of a Mrs Richardson. Mrs Richardson had remarried a vicar and was now Mrs Butterfield. Harriet's problem was that she was educationally subnormal, could not write, and had difficulty in reading. She had, however, a stubborn streak and was a minor heiress. After a few run-ins with her mother, in 1874 Harriet had decided to leave home and live with her aunt, a Mrs Ellis, in Walworth. She was 33.

Harriet met a couple, the Hinckmans. Mrs Hinckman had been a Mrs Rhodes and was the mother of Alice and Mrs Patrick Staunton. It was bound to happen that Patrick Staunton's unmarried brother, Louis, an auctioneer's clerk, and, at a mere 24, some years younger than Harriet, would sniff an opportunity when he visited his sister-in-law's family. He courted the naïve, trusting but socially superior Harriet and married her in Clapham on 24 June 1875. His marriage ensured that her monies, the then princely sum of £1,600, reverted to him. He was later to cash in on more, another £2,000. Her mother tried to stop the marriage by applying for Harriet to become a ward of Chancery, but was unable to do so.

The Stauntons moved to 8 Loughborough Park Road, Brixton, where the fretful mother made an abortive attempt to speak to her daughter, but was firmly told by Mr Staunton to keep away. The Stauntons then moved to 8 Colby Road, Gypsy Hill in 1876, as did Alice Rhodes, Mrs Patrick Staunton's sister and Clara Brown, a maid-of-all-work. Louis Staunton set himself up as an estate agent with some of the proceeds of his wife's inheritance. It did not prove successful, as he rarely made an appearance in his office.

It was in Gypsy Hill that Harriet started to suspect that her husband was having an affair with Alice Rhodes. He was. Harriet's temper frayed, their son Thomas Henry Staunton was born and Louis started openly living with Alice Rhodes.

Louis's brother, Patrick, an artist, moved to Cudham in Kent, some 8 miles from Bromley, in 1875. In 1876 Harriet and her infant went to visit them. Louis and Patrick came to an arrangement that she could stay with them for a £1 weekly fee, while he moved in with Alice to another cottage on the other side of the village. A useful little arrangement: one brother could get rid of an unwanted wife and the other could benefit from a little income. Alice Rhodes even passed herself off as Mrs Louis Staunton. The Patrick Stauntons, meanwhile, kept Harriet virtually confined to her room.

The increasingly worried Mrs Butterfield had found out that the Stauntons were living in the Cudham area and that Louis seemed to have taken up with another woman. Louis heard the rumours that his mother-in-law was looking for her daughter and wrote her a letter, postmarked from Brighton, warning her off and telling her that her daughter did not want to see her again. Mrs Butterfield's fears were further fuelled when she unexpectedly met Alice Rhodes at London Bridge station wearing some of her daughter's jewellery. She started thinking the worst. She did travel to Cudham, but had to beat a hasty retreat.

Little Thomas Staunton was taken to Guy's Hospital on 8 April 1877, more dead than alive. He died the same day and was registered as Henry Stormton. Patrick Staunton, posing as a Mr Harris, arranged the burial. The child's mother was also deteriorating fast.

On that fateful 12 April the two brothers and Mrs Patrick Staunton went up to Penge to arrange for a flat for a very sick lady who could eat but wouldn't. They maintained, according to their landlady, Mrs Chalklin, that they needed to get better medical advice. The virtually unconscious Harriet was half-carried from the train and taken to the flat where she later died.

Clara Brown's candid statements in court proved the Stauntons' undoing. She told the court that Louis Staunton started having an affair with Alice Rhodes almost as soon as she came to live with them. His wife suspected, but he shouted her down, beat her occasionally and shut her in her room. He once gave her a black eye when she questioned him too closely about the sale of her only property. He managed to browbeat her into signing it away. As to her stay with Patrick Staunton, Clara Brown stated that Patrick had hit Harriet several times and even gave her short rations, sometimes not even bothering to feed her.

On the seventh day, 26 September 1877, Mr Justice Hawkins summed up. It took 10½ hours. The jury deliberated for just under an hour and a half. All the defendants were guilty of murder. The judge ordered that they should be hanged.

The executions were set for Tuesday 16 October, in Maidstone Gaol. Judge Hawkins had, however, openly contested the doctors' evidence at the trial. This evidence suggested that Harriet may well have died of meningitis. The medical establishment penned, en masse, an open letter to the Home Secretary. Their conclusions were that the post-mortem evidence, combined with the statements made about the physical and mental attitude of the deceased, showed that it was a deterioration of mental faculties – meningitis – that precipitated the death, not starvation.

Lord Cross, the Home Secretary, reopened the case in the light of this evidence. The death penalties were revoked on 14 October. Alice Rhodes received a free pardon, while the other three had their sentences commuted to penal servitude for life.

There was no doubt that Louis Staunton married for money. There was no doubt he bided his time. Whether or not the brothers actively engineered Harriet's early demise could never be successfully established.

17

THE RICHMOND MYSTERY

*The murder of Julia Martha Thomas,
Richmond, 1879*

It was early morning, 5 March 1879. Henry Wheatley, a coal porter at the Old George Inn, Mortlake, was trundling his cart, with a passenger, along the banks of the Thames. Passing opposite Barnes Terrace, about 30yd from the bridge, he noticed a large wooden box half submerged in the water. Curious, he stopped the horse and, with the help of his friend, dragged the large box out of the water onto the bank. He cut the cord around it and opened it. He might have expected to find an infant, because there had been quite a few instances of unwanted children boxed and drowned in the Thames. Instead, his eyes fell on what seemed to be a huge mass of cooked flesh.

Wheatley ran to Barnes police station, alerted Inspector Harber, and helped him to carry the heavy box back to the station. Dr Adams, a local doctor, viewed the grisly contents and confirmed that it was indeed flesh – human flesh. He also thought it had been boiled. Unfortunately there was no chance of identifying the mass because the head and one foot were missing. The inquest on the findings led to an open verdict, although the papers surmised that it might have been medical student japes, or worse – murder.

On 9 March the inhabitants of Park Road, Richmond, were called to their doors by the cries of a newspaper boy: 'Supposed murder; shocking discovery of human remains found in a box on the Thames.' Mrs Porter, visiting her friend Mrs Thomas at 2 Vine Cottages (otherwise known as Mayfield Cottages), recoiled in horror, but Kate Thomas went to the boy and bought a paper from him, laughing about it.

For John Church, landlord and owner of the Rising Sun public house, Rose Gardens, Hammersmith, 18 March 1879 was a busy day. Indeed, he thought it might even be a very profitable one. He had recently been introduced to a widow, Mrs Kate Thomas, by his good friends the Porters. She wanted to sell all the furniture in a house in Richmond that she had recently inherited

No. 2 Mayfield Cottages, Richmond. *(P.G. de Loriol)*

from an aunt. The lady seemed to be about 35, not remotely pretty, almost manlike, but she had a way about her that made him leave his wife at home to ferret through Mrs Thomas's charming house at Vine Cottages for days on end. It was those extraordinary eyes, the slight Irish lilt, those white teeth, and a certain wildness about her that gave her a disquieting, but not unpleasing allure.

He was at 2 Vine Cottages, supervising the last of the packing and removals of all the effects he was interested in, when an elderly lady called over from the next house. Miss Elizabeth Ives explained she was Mrs Thomas's landlady. What was Mr Church doing? He was removing all Mrs Thomas's chattels, as requested by her. Where was she? She was inside somewhere, he thought. He went inside to tell Mrs Thomas. She would deal with this. Meanwhile would he take all the silk dresses and pack them with the furniture? He did just that and left, but not before giving her £18 for the furniture. She told him she would see him later.

A few hours later Mrs Thomas arrived at the Rising Sun in high dudgeon. She seemed to be in a rush, and begged a sovereign off him – she would return it after she had been to see her family.

After a couple of days of mulling things over, Mr Church thought there was something slightly odd about that last day with Mrs Thomas. Maria Church thought he ought to check the furniture – it might give him a clue as to Mrs Thomas's whereabouts. It didn't, but Mrs Church's search through the silk dresses discovered something disquieting. A letter revealed that the owner of one dress was a certain Kate Webster. The letter was from her uncle, writing from Killane in Ireland. Slight alarm bells rang. Another letter was from a Mr Charles Menhennick of Finsbury Park to Mrs Thomas.

Armed with the two letters and accompanied by Mr Porter, Mr Church went to see Mr Menhennick. Mr Menhennick told them that Mrs Thomas

was an elderly lady and a friend of the family. Mr Menhennick then contacted Mrs Thomas's solicitor, Mr Hughes. Mr Hughes was indisposed, but his brother called on the Churches on 22 March to find out what was going on. He and Mr Church then went to Richmond police station, and its inspector, Mr Pearman, accompanied them to 2 Vine Cottages.

Inspector Pearman visited Mr Church the following day. Church sent for Robert Porter, his friend's son, who told Pearman that on 2 March he and Mrs Thomas had carried a very heavy box to Richmond Bridge. He couldn't forget that box because it was missing a handle and it hurt his hand. On seeing it at Richmond police station, Robert recognised the box immediately.

The police lost no time in sending out Kate Webster's description. It was now patently obvious that Kate had masqueraded as the woman she had killed. She was arrested at Killane on 28 March. The London police had been busy. Kate was a known felon. In fact, she had been in and out of prison ever since she had come to England in about 1865. Her speciality was robbing lodging houses, but now she had gone one better – she had murdered, and what a murder it was! The landlady of her local inn, the Hole in the Wall, could not believe that Kate had been talking to her while Mrs Thomas was being boiled in a vat in her own cottage!

Kate Webster. *(P.G. de Loriol)*

Kate Webster was returned to London. Her sordid life was exposed. She had had a son, born in 1874 and looked after since January 1879 by a friend, Mrs Crease. In January the jobless Kate had been introduced to an old lady of the parish, Mrs Thomas. Mrs Thomas, a lady of about 55, was down on her luck, had been through two husbands, and was regarded as a bit of an eccentric.

Despite Kate having no adequate references, Mrs Thomas accepted her offer to work for her. Mrs Thomas was quite strict with servants, but in Kate she had met her match. Mrs Thomas had fine dresses and pretty jewellery.

She was genteel, fanatical about cleanliness, as well as prim and a bit of a martinet. Kate was rugged, clumsy, slapdash, strong, and hard as nails – until it came to her boy. It was not a partnership made in heaven. Mrs Thomas grew to fear Kate in the few short days Kate was with her. One argument too many, and she gave Kate her marching orders – notice to leave on 28 February 1879. Kate, however, managed to wangle a few extra days.

Mrs Thomas went to church on Sunday 3 March. An old servant thought she looked out of sorts. She was the last person to report having seen her alive. Mrs Thomas then returned to Vine Cottages only to have another argument with Kate.

What exactly happened will never be known, but in the next hour Kate killed her employer, laid her out on the kitchen table, and dismembered her, boiling her up in a large pan. She disposed of one foot in the river and the head also disappeared. In the next couple of days she attempted to sell jars of fat to neighbours – one wonders what the cooking fat was . . .

On Tuesday 4 March Kate arrived, with a very heavy bag, at the house of Mr and Mrs Porter of Rose Gardens, Hammersmith. They had known her in 1873 when she had lived in the same area. Now they were confronted with a very different Kate from the dishevelled one they once knew. She wore an expensive dress, pretty jewellery, and spoke much better. She had, she explained, married a Mr Thomas. He had died and she had inherited an aunt's house in Richmond and wanted to sell the furniture, as she was moving to be nearer her family in Scotland. Could they recommend someone?

Meanwhile, she asked whether their son Robert could help her back to Richmond, and on the way she could drop off her bag at a friend's. She would pay for his return journey. Naturally, they were only too pleased to help. Robert carried her very heavy bag to Barnes. She took it from him, and returned promptly after delivering it. They then went back to 2 Vine Cottages, collected a large and cumbersome box, and walked down to Richmond Bridge where the box was, according to Kate, safely delivered – although Robert and a passer-by had heard a splash.

Kate Webster was charged with wilfully murdering Mrs Thomas and stealing her furniture. She was committed for trial before Mr Justice Denman at the Central Criminal Court on 2 July 1879. The 'guilty' verdict was returned on 8 July, but not before Kate had pleaded pregnancy – a plea dismissed by a panel of matrons.

She was hanged at Wandsworth on 29 July 1879. Mr Church, as ever looking for a bargain, bought most of Mrs Thomas's belongings at an auction at her house. One woman bought Mrs Thomas's bed, the bed Kate had slept in for at least a couple of nights after her mistress's death. Once money had been exchanged the purchaser turned to a young woman next to her and said loudly 'there, that's for you to sleep in'. The rest of the company laughed with her.

18

RUN FOR THE MONEY

The murder of Percy John, Wimbledon, 1881

Percy Malcolm John was an unfortunate soul. He had been declared a ward in Chancery after his parents had died in 1870. The then 7-year-old was the youngest in a family of five. He was also crippled – he had a curvature of the spine and was confined to a wheelchair throughout his life.

But fortune had smiled on him. He went to a boarding school in Wimbledon – Blenheim House, run by a Mr William Henry Bedbrook – in 1879. The school was within a minute's walk of Wimbledon station and was perfect for the young Percy. He was happy there. His surviving sisters had married well – Margaret to a clerk in the Civil Service, William Chapman, who became Percy's guardian, and Kate to the eminent Dr George Henry Lamson. Lamson looked after the youth's medical welfare. Percy was to inherit £3,000 on his eighteenth birthday. Should he die before his twenty-first birthday the money would pass to his sisters.

On Saturday 3 December 1881 the contented Percy was expecting his dear brother-in-law at the school. He was excited about his birthday, 19 December, his holidays the day after and his brother-in-law's visit. He and his brother-in-law were very close. Dr Lamson had written to him to expect his visit on that day – it would be a fleeting one, because Lamson was going to Paris, and then to Florence, to visit his father. The Principal, Mr Bedbrook, had declared this Saturday to be a holiday and the senior boys, who had just taken their exams, were readying the school for a party that evening, organised by the Principal.

Dr George Henry Lamson. *(P.G. de Loriol)*

Mr Bedbrook was the first to see Lamson. He barely recognised him. The 32-year-old looked worn and haggard. He took him into the dining room while Percy was fetched. They talked about the exams that Percy had recently done. Percy, in his chair, was then rolled in. Percy was shocked by his brother-in-law's appearance and said as much; Lamson replied that Percy looked very well indeed. Mr Bedbrook gave his guest a glass of sherry. Dr Lamson asked for some sugar, poured it into his sherry and gulped it down in one mouthful. He then opened his Gladstone bag and took out a bottle of sweets, some crystallised fruits and a Dundee cake. Mr Bedbrook watched while Lamson cut the cake with his penknife and offered a piece each to his brother-in-law and to the Principal. They both ate their portions. Lamson then reached into his bag again and brought out some gelatine capsules which, he said, he had got in America. They were very good for taking nauseous medicines in. He asked the Principal to try one. He did, noticing that even in his hand the capsule started to melt. Percy also took the capsule handed to him by Lamson. Bedbrook noticed that it seemed to be filled with some white, powdery substance. The two men then talked about the school. The Doctor then said that he was taking a train to Paris that evening and needed to go. Mr Bedbrook accompanied him to the front door and spoke briefly with him about Percy – his curvature seemed to be getting worse. Dr Lamson suspected the youth had not long to live.

Meanwhile, Percy reflected on the too-short visit of his brother-in-law. He felt a bit down. Mr Bedbrook noticed this and brought two young women to cheer him up. Young Percy was soon playing at the piano, accompanied by the singing girls. They had to cut things short as the evening party was starting.

When the Principal next saw Percy, the boy complained of heartburn, a bit he said, like the last time his brother-in-law had given him a quinine pill at Shanklin. Bedbrook asked Percy's room-mate to carry him to bed, and asked Mrs Bowles, the matron, to keep an eye on the lad.

At about 8.30 p.m. Mrs Bowles found Percy vomiting in the bathroom. He complained that his throat was burning and that he found it difficult to breathe. Spasms were wracking his body. Mrs Bowles and a master undressed him and put him to bed. She gave Percy some brandy to settle his stomach and then went to see Mr Bedbrook.

Shortly before nine o'clock Dr Berry, the school's doctor, arrived for the party. He was hurried off to see Percy. The doctor tried pouring white of egg mixed with water down the boy's throat, and applied linseed poultices to his stomach, but Percy's spasms became even worse. Dr Berry could make neither head nor tail of it. Bedbrook suggested that Dr Little, another of his evening's guests, should be brought up to give a second opinion. Berry thought this a good idea. Both doctors thought they could try morphine. Some was injected into the boy's stomach, but it only stopped the spasms for an hour. Percy asked for more. He was given more and fell asleep. The doctors then noticed that his heart rate was slow and his breathing more shallow. They tried to revive him, but he died at 11.20 p.m. without having woken up.

Conscious of post-mortem requirements, the doctors scraped the vomit from the bathroom floor and bottled it. The next morning Mr Bedbrook visited the local police station to report Percy's death. He gave a statement to Inspector Fuller and gave him the capsules, the crystallised fruit and the Dundee cake left by Dr Lamson. Suspicion immediately fell on Lamson.

The post-mortem was on Tuesday 6 December. Drs Little and Berry, assisted by Mr Bond FRCS, did the examination. Mr Bond, on seeing the condition of the stomach, was quite sure that the boy had been poisoned.

The *Evening Standard* of 6 December was full of the news, including the suspicions that Dr Lamson had done the deed. Scotland Yard received a letter from Dr Lamson the next day saying that he had read the *Standard*, denied the allegations and would come to Scotland Yard the following day to confront the police.

Dr Lamson arrived at Scotland Yard with his wife. Inspector Butcher was surprised to see in his office the man whom he had asked a constable to find in Paris! Dr Lamson said that he wished to clear things up. He would be in Chichester for the next few days, and he gave his address, but before he could leave Inspector Butcher arrested him for Percy's murder. Dr Lamson took this calmly and asked for the fact that he had come to the police of his own volition to be taken into consideration. It would be.

The trial began on Wednesday 8 March 1882 and lasted six days. The courtroom at the Old Bailey was packed. Justice Hawkins, later Lord Brampton, presided; Sir Henry Poland appeared for the prosecution and Montagu

The Old Bailey. (*P.G. de Loriol*)

Sir Henry Hawkins (1817–1907). *(P.G. de Loriol)*

Williams for the defence. It was established, from the contents of the victim's stomach, that Percy had died of aconitine poisoning – a particularly virulent and fatal poison.

It is very difficult to trace aconitine, otherwise known as Wolf's Bane or Monk's Hood, in the system. The symptoms are a burning sensation on the lips, tightening of the throat, a growing sense of strangulation which obstructs breathing, violent abdominal pains and vomiting. Then the pulse weakens and breathing becomes shallow and spasmodic. Finally the respiratory functions are paralysed and death is caused by asphyxia some four hours after administration. These were the symptoms that Percy had showed.

Lamson pleaded 'not guilty'. His dutiful wife paid for his counsel. Williams was a master of defence, but Poland successfully argued that it was poison that had killed the victim, poison that had been administered by the defendant. A raisin skin impregnated with aconitine was found in the deceased's stomach. This could only have come from the Dundee cake. But Mr Bedbrook had seen the doctor cutting it – maybe he had pre-cut the slice he had given to his brother-in-law and had only pretended to cut it in his presence.

Although Williams was persuaded that Lamson had murdered Percy, he needed to show that his mind was unbalanced in order to try to save his client's life. Lamson's sad life was brought to the public's attention. There had been insanity in his American father's family for at least two generations as his grandmother, great uncle and aunt had all ended up in Columbia Asylum. Lamson himself had shown childhood tendencies to 'mental disturbances from slight causes'. His career was marred by near-incompetence although his entry in the Medical Directory read like a hero's:

Lamson, George Henry, 'Hursley', Poole Road, Bournemouth, Hants – M.D. Paris, 1870; L.R.C.P Edin. and L.M., 1878 (Paris, Vienna, Pennsylvan. and Lond.); Mem. Brit. Med. Assoc. and Bournemouth Med. Assoc.; Med. Ref. Wesl. and several other Assur. Socs.; Sen. Asst. Surg. French Ambulance Corps, 1870–71 (Bronze and Iron Crosses); Surg. Servian Army (British Red Cross), 1876–77 (Gold Cross and Medal): Surg. Maj. Russian Serv., and Chief Surg. Costaforo Eng. Milit. Hosp., Bucharest, 1877–78 (Ord. Star of Roumania 4th class and Ord. Medjidie 5th Class); formerly Externe Surg. Matern. Hosp. Paris.

One medical student during the Franco-Prussian War had said that Lamson took offence over imagined injuries and constantly railed about the state of the theatres. During the siege of Paris his ministrations were considered a greater threat to patients than the Germans. He could not be trusted to administer medicines. A colleague at the Red Cross Hospital in Bucharest concluded that he was of unsound mind and wholly irresponsible for his conduct. The same colleague also remembered how Lamson had boasted of his adventures in the American Civil War – but he was only 12 at the time.

Dr Lamson became wholly dependent on morphine and atropine in 1877 and his world spiralled into a complete haze. He lost most of the patients in his Bournemouth practice, and most of his wife's inheritance from her brother, Hubert John's death – that in itself was suspicious. He also wrote worthless cheques. Desperate for money to finance his habit, he resorted to a final inheritance – and for that his brother-in-law needed to die.

The jury's verdict was 'guilty'. Lamson made his will while they deliberated. He was due to hang on 2 April 1882, but representations were made on his behalf from America. He was finally executed on 28 April 1882 at Wandsworth Prison, having made a full confession to the Prison Chaplain beforehand.

Lamson was destroyed by his obsession – drugs. More important, it destroyed his wife and daughter. Although no concrete proof was given at the trial as to how the poison was administered, he was sentenced to hang.

19

TRUST ME, I'M A DOCTOR

Thomas Neill Cream, serial murderer, Lambeth, 1891

Despite the mushrooming redevelopments trying to cater for a city bursting at its seams, the area surrounding Waterloo retains its industrial past where more than one industry held sway. This was one of the largest red-light districts of London where young women plied their trade from dingy backstreets.

James Styles was standing outside the Wellington Pub in Waterloo Road (SE1) on the evening of 13 October 1891 when he saw a young woman collapse on the other side of the road. He rushed over, helped her up, took her address – 8 Duke (now Duchy) Street – and helped the trembling, twitching young woman home. The girl was one of the many prostitutes who plied their trade in the area.

During a pause in her dramatic convulsions the 19-year-old Ellen Donworth told her landlady and Inspector Harvey of the Lambeth Division that a 'tall gentleman with cross eyes, a silk hat, and bushy whiskers gave me a drink twice out of a bottle with white stuff in it'. She had met him previously. He had sent her two letters which he had asked to be returned when she saw him last. Mr Johnson, of the South London Medical Institute, diagnosed that her convulsions were of the type caused by an overdose of strychnine. She was rushed to St Thomas's Hospital, where she died in agony. A post-mortem revealed a quarter of a grain of strychnine in her stomach. The 'Lambeth Mystery' caused a 'fearful sensation in South Lambeth'. A strange letter demanding £300,000 in exchange for information on the murderer of Miss Donworth was received by the Deputy Coroner, Mr George Wyatt. He filed it. The inquest gave a verdict of death by poisoning with strychnine and morphia by a person unknown.

Matilda Clover, 27 years old, lived in lodgings at 27 Lambeth Road (SE1) with her 2-year-old boy. She was a pleasant-faced young woman, beginning to be ravaged by alcoholism. On 19 October 1891 one of her housemates

Houses in Waterloo Bridge Road. *(Old and New London)*

St Thomas's Hospital. *(P.G. de Loriol)*

noticed a letter addressed to Matilda, asking her to meet the writer the following night, bringing the letter with her. It was signed 'Fred'.

Matilda went out on the evening of 20 October, and returned with a tall, moustached, heavily built man. He wore a large coat, a silk hat and glasses. He left late. At about three in the morning the household was woken by screams of agony. Everybody rushed to Matilda's room. She said that Fred had given her some pills. Mr Coppin, an assistant to Dr McCarthy of Westminster Bridge Road, thought her fits were due to chronic alcohol poisoning. She died in agony. On 21 October her doctor, Dr Graham, ascribed her death to alcohol poisoning. Matilda was buried in Tooting cemetery on 27 October.

On 6 November Messrs W.H. Smith & Son, of 186 The Strand, received an extraordinary letter claiming that Mr F.W.D. Smith was the murderer of Ellen Donworth. Countess Russell, who was staying at the Savoy, received a letter accusing her husband of murdering Matilda Clover by poison. The esteemed Dr Broadbent, of Seymour Street (W1), received a blackmail letter on 30 November accusing him of the murder of Matilda Clover. He handed it to the police – he thought it was the work of a lunatic. The papers reported nothing on murders in South London for the next few months. The Waterloo area was quiet. The prostitutes plied their trade from Stamford Street (SE1) and other nearby streets.

PC George Cumley of the Lambeth Division was walking his beat at 2.15 a.m. on 12 April. As he passed down Stamford Street he noticed that a young woman was seeing a large, bespectacled, moustached man out of No. 118. The man, in tall silk hat and cape, disappeared towards Waterloo Road. PC Cumley's return beat brought him back to the house forty-five minutes later. A cab stood outside No. 118, as did one of his colleagues, PC Eversfield. Eversfield had a bundle in his arms. It was the girl Cumley had seen earlier, Emma Shrivell, an 18-year-old prostitute. Eversfield explained that he had been called by the landlord, George Vogt. Both Shrivell and her 21-year-old friend, Alice Marsh, had woken the house with their screams. Cumley carried Alice Marsh down the stairs to the waiting cab. He established that the girls had been given three pills by their customer 'Fred' – the man he had seen.

Alice Marsh died on the way to St Thomas's; Shrivell died six hours later. The police began to become suspicious that a serial murderer was at work. They had Matilda Clover's body exhumed – she had died of strychnine poisoning.

On 26 April Dr Joseph Harper of Barnstaple received a letter claiming that his son, a medical student at St Thomas's, was the murderer of the two girls of Stamford Street. The writer also said that the information could be suppressed on the payment of £1,500. Meanwhile John Haynes, erstwhile engineer and part-time secret agent, lodger of Mr and Mrs Armstead of 129 Westminster Bridge Road, was introduced to a balding, large, myopic man, a friend of his landlord, a certain Dr Neill of Canada. As both men had been to America they seemed to have much in common, although Dr Neill's rather lurid accounts of some of his adventures made Haynes aware that there was something more to this rather eccentric bull of a man.

Haynes would sometimes walk across Westminster Bridge to see his friend, Detective Inspector McIntyre of Scotland Yard, and chatted to him, among other things, of this curious new acquaintance of his, Dr Neill.

Constable Cumley had described the man he had seen at 118 Stamford Street to Sergeant Ward. On the evening of 12 May, his sergeant called for Cumley to meet him on Westminster Bridge Road. He pointed to a pub on the corner of Lambeth Palace Road. There was the man Cumley had seen. The man started to follow a prostitute. They followed him at a discreet distance, down St George's Road, then into a house on Elliott's Row. They waited, and followed his return to 103 Lambeth Palace Road. It was decided that the gentleman should be discreetly tailed. Neill found this out.

Dr Neill told his friend, John Haynes, that he was being watched. Haynes, in turn, asked McIntyre whether the police were observing his friend Dr Neill – McIntyre was non-committal. Dr Neill then took his friend out for lunch and told him that he was sure one of the other lodgers at 103 Lambeth Palace

Road, a young medical student, Walter Harper, was the murderer of Ellen Donworth, Matilda Clover, Alice Marsh, Emma Shrivell and one Lou Harvey. The medical student had asked Dr Neill's advice. The astounded Haynes wrote the details in his notebook.

Inspector McIntyre was just leaving the Armsteads' home when he was accosted by Neill, who was on his way to see Haynes. Neill explained he was a travelling salesman and resented being followed by the police. Would McIntyre look into it? He did, and discovered Cumley's statement about the man seen leaving 118 Stamford Street. McIntyre visited Dr Neill at his lodgings, requested and was given a list of his movements while in the country – which omitted, however, his account of the day of the Stamford Street murders. Simultaneously the police searched for the mysterious Lou Harvey who, Neill said, had been murdered – but to no avail.

On 26 May Neill wrote, through his solicitors, to the Chief Commissioner of Police, Sir Edward Bradford, complaining he was being shadowed and it was affecting his business. Inspector Tunbridge of the CID was instructed to look into the South Lambeth poisoning cases. He visited Dr Neill and was shown a medical case containing, among other bottles, a bottle of strychnine grains. Tunbridge also visited Dr Harper and realised that the blackmail letter was in Neill's handwriting. They could nail Neill for blackmail!

Neill – protesting his innocence – was arrested on 3 June and the following day was charged at Bow Street Magistrates' Court with attempting to extort money. The accused was represented by John E. Waters and Bernard Thomas represented the Treasury. Tunbridge paid another visit to Neill's lodgings and discovered a wealth of information.

Dr Thomas Neill Cream.
(P.G. de Loriol)

Matilda Clover's inquest opened on 22 June. It was established that Dr Neill was in fact a Dr Thomas Neill Cream. He had been seen entering the deceased's premises on the day she had died. Her death was now confirmed as being by strychnine poisoning. Dr Cream was charged and was tried at the Old Bailey on 17 October 1892.

He was formally indicted for four murders and other crimes. There was no hard evidence for these, but the Crown rested its case on the cumulative evidence. The jury took a few minutes to return a verdict of 'guilty'.

The life story of Thomas Neill Cream gradually unfolded. Born in Glasgow in 1850, he had emigrated with his family to Canada, where the bright adolescent studied medicine at McGill University. After gaining his degree he performed back-street abortions and was certainly involved in at least two murders – he

The Spider's Web.
(P.G. de Loriol)

was charged with second degree murder for one of these, and spent some time in prison. He also relied on a constant supply of morphine to alleviate the pains caused by a bad squint. Early on he interested himself in the powers of strychnine. His move to England in 1891 followed his father's death and his own release from prison. He could now continue his seedy life relatively unknown. Had he not sent the letters, he might never have been brought to book, but his need for constant attention produced the outcome he least expected – or did it?

He was hanged at Newgate on 15 November 1892. His supposed last words were 'I am Jack . . .', cut short by the rope. This led to his being a suspect in the 'Ripper' murders, although his claim was never really taken seriously.

20

DEATH OF A FIANCÉE

*The murder of Elizabeth Camp,
South London, 1897*

The date 11 February 1897 was a wonderful day for Elizabeth Camp. She had visited her younger sister in Hammersmith in the morning and arrived in Hounslow at 5 p.m. in time for tea with her elder sister, Mrs Haynes. She had shopped until she dropped, for her wedding day, in both Hammersmith and Hounslow. Edward Berry, her fiancé, would be meeting her in the booking hall at Waterloo station at 8.25 p.m. From there they would go to a music hall and then he would escort her home.

Elizabeth was in a bit of a rush. Her sister and a family friend had bought her a drink to toast the future bride and time had just flown past. None of them had looked at the clock, and it had been a rush to get to the station and board the train, despite her sister and a kindly porter telling her that there was plenty of time for her to catch her waiting train; she rushed down the platform as if the hounds of hell were at her heels.

Elizabeth Camp was a very self-possessed 33-year-old, 13st woman. In her young teens she had worked as a barmaid at the Good Intent public house; she had then become a nurse at Winchmore Hill and later returned to the pub as manageress.

Sure enough, Edward, a Walworth fruiterer, was waiting for his intended at Waterloo station. Despite his Lizzie's common sense, he always fretted about her. He was looking forward to seeing her this evening, as they were going to discuss the arrangements for the wedding.

The train arrived bang on time. Edward watched as the passengers disgorged from it and waited. He waited until 8.35 p.m., and still no Lizzie. Impatiently he went to the platform, but the ticket collector told him that the passengers had long since gone. He was just about to leave the platform when he saw a small crowd and a couple of policemen gathering around one of the carriage doors. He approached and asked what was going on.

A carriage cleaner walking down the train had discovered some legs protruding from underneath the seat of a second-class carriage. They belonged to the body of a woman. Edward had a dreadful premonition. It

Waterloo station, 1905. *(National Railway Museum/Science & Society Picture Library)*

was only after the body had been placed on a stretcher and carted off to St Thomas's Hospital, and Edward had been asked to identify the body, that his whole world fell apart. Elizabeth's head was badly smashed and there had been blood all over the carriage. The cause of death was a blow from a blunt instrument. A pair of bone cufflinks was found close to the body and the dead woman didn't seem to have a ticket.

None of the woman's jewellery was missing. She had put up a good fight. Her purse, however, was missing, and it was known that she had had a ticket. Was her assailant a sex-fiend? Why did her assailant pick on a train with so few passengers and billed to stop at quite a few railway stations barely five minutes apart? Why pick on a strong woman rather than on an easier victim?

Detective Chief Inspector Marshall headed the investigation. He and his team noted that Elizabeth's blood was still warm when her body reached St Thomas's, so she must have been murdered during the last few stops and the killer must have alighted at one of these stops, if he hadn't got off at

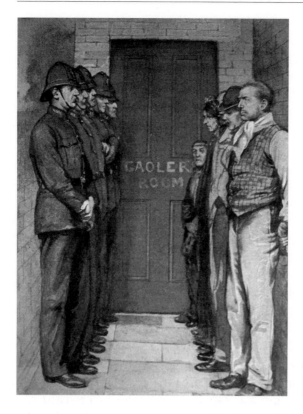

Awaiting ordeal.
(Living London, *George R. Sim*,
Cassell & Co., 1901)

Waterloo. They checked the last few stations. The railway staff had seen no
suspicious people, nor had they noticed blood on anybody.

The breakthrough came during a search of the tracks. Midway between
Wandsworth and Putney, the searching police found a porcelain pestle
matted with brown hair and congealed blood. Photos of the pestle were
released to the press and an appeal was launched for all who had travelled
on the train. The very next day a man came forward to say that he had seen
a frock-coated, dark-moustached man, wearing a top hat, get off the train at
Wandsworth on the night in question. An all-points bulletin was issued to the
press and a mentally unstable man introduced himself to a railway official at
Wandsworth, claiming he was the killer.

There were no more leads. The inquest opened on 17 February at Lambeth
Coroner's Court. The only 'new information' was wholly owing to police
enthusiasm.

A young man, Arthur Marshall, a ne'er-do-well by his mother's account,
had disappeared from his home in Reading on 11 February, but had returned
on the night of the 15th. Mrs Marshall had reported his disappearance and
police investigations had found that he had gone to Guildford and, under an
assumed name, purchased a false moustache from a costumier's. It was only
after a very severe interrogation that he owned up to thinking of joining the

army in an effort to mend his ways. He had purchased a moustache to make him look older – but he had then given up.

The jury foreman did ask one very salient question before the inquest broke up for a month. Why was it that the Railway Company had not put up a reward for information? The North London Railway had offered £100 for information leading to the killer of a Mr Briggs.

Had the killer's blows been delivered during a chance encounter, or by someone known to Elizabeth Camp? Edward Berry hadn't been the first man in Miss Camp's life. She had been engaged to a barman at the Portman Arms, a man called Brown. The engagement had been broken off because of a violent argument. Brown was also intensely jealous and Elizabeth had recently received some threatening letters. She was very good with money and seemed to have saved rather a lot, whereas Brown was totally inept where money was concerned. The police were heartened by this new information, but it was to be demolished.

Brown had an unshakeable alibi on the night in question and it was he, not Elizabeth, who had broken the engagement. He, however, had heard that she was receiving flowers from a mysterious stranger who waited for her outside the Good Intent. But the potential lead proved to be yet another dead end.

On further investigation it seemed that quite a few individuals owed Miss Camp money, including her younger sister's husband (whom she had seen in Hammersmith on her last day) and the 'family friend' who had toasted her impending wedding in Hounslow – a Mr Thomas Stone. The police thought he might be the missing man.

The police had met so many dead ends in their investigation that they were winding it down. The bone cufflinks had been borrowed from her sister; the moustachioed man could never be found; the pestle remained a mystery; the Hammersmith brother-in-law, manager of a store, lived far above his income, but this didn't come to much; and finally there was the friend, Mr Thomas Stone.

Mr Stone was taken to Hounslow police station and questioned. He had disappeared from Hounslow for some four hours on that fateful day, but still the police hadn't enough information to charge him. That was the last of the Waterloo affair.

On the final day of the adjourned inquest, 7 April 1897, the jury returned a verdict of 'wilful murder against some person or persons unknown'. The police had their suspicions. Fingerprinting, a science that would come to the fore in less than a decade, was still in its infancy, unfortunately.

Walworth turned out in full force for Elizabeth's funeral. One hundred and fifty mounted police were on duty to control the crowds. She was buried in Walworth cemetery. A *Times* reporter recorded 'three mourning coaches, fifteen carriages, cabs and other vehicles, and five omnibuses, the latter crowded with mourners'.

21

WAS HE, WASN'T HE?

The murder of Maud Marsh,
Borough, 1902

Maud Marsh thought she was lucky when she landed a job as a barmaid at the Monument Tavern in Borough, in August 1901. She found the landlord, the 37-year-old George Chapman, charming. Those dark, brooding looks of his, his fine, long moustache and his undoubted sex appeal were hard to resist. She couldn't, and ended up in his bed, followed by marriage.

George was masterful. George was brutal. George beat her without a break. She confided to her sister on a bus journey in Streatham that 'You don't know what he is'. Her parents visited her from Croydon. They didn't like George. Then Maud started suffering strange symptoms: headaches, nausea, vomiting and diarrhoea. Her parents insisted that she go to hospital. She was taken to Guy's, where her illness was diagnosed as peritonitis. She recovered and returned to her duties. Unfortunately, Maud's illness recurred. A Dr Stoker visited. Then George took over a new pub, the Crown, where Dr Stoker again attended her. Maud's condition got no better.

Her parents visited her frequently. Her sister also nursed her. Her father's suspicions made him consult his own doctor in Croydon, describing the symptoms and telling him about Chapman's insistence on preparing all Maud's meals and medicines. The doctor visited Maud on 21 October. George Chapman wasn't pleased but couldn't stop him. What the doctor saw alarmed him. He decided that Maud was being poisoned and that he would visit Dr Stoker the next day.

On 22 October 1902 Maud died, wracked with pain. A doctor was called to issue a death certificate, but without having seen the patient before and not being able to diagnose the illness, he wisely refused.

At the insistence of the girl's family a post-mortem examination was carried out, and 7.24 grains of antimony and traces of arsenic were found throughout Maud's body. Inspector Godfrey arrested George Chapman on 25 October.

While Chapman was in custody the police started to make enquiries. They questioned Dr Stoker. Mr Chapman had been married before. His previous wife, the 36-year-old Bessie Taylor, had died at the Monument Tavern on

13 February 1901 from 'exhaustion from vomiting and diarrhoea'. She had suffered beatings, too. She had been buried in her home town of Lymm in Cheshire. Chapman had previously been a landlord of the Prince of Wales pub, off City Road in Bartholomew Square, and his then wife, Mary Isabella Spink, had fallen ill and died on 25 December 1897. The local doctor, Dr Rodgers, had prescribed medicines which Chapman had prepared himself. The two women who nursed Mrs Spink, Elizabeth Waymark and Martha Doubleday, told the prosecutor that the body was a mere skeleton. Doubleday also said that Chapman had broken down and cried when his wife died, then opened the pub as usual. Further investigations revealed that Chapman had bought some tartar emetic, a powerful poison, from a chemist on 3 April 1897.

The big break came when the police delved further and found that George Chapman and a certain Severin Antoniovich Klosowski were one and the same person. Klosowski was from Poland and had arrived in England in 1887–8. He had studied surgery in Poland for five years and had a good record as a surgeon. On arrival in England he had become an assistant barber near the East India Docks, then Cable Street, Commercial Street and Greenfield Street in the East End, where he was a fully fledged barber. He had married a fellow Pole, Lucy Baderski, only to be hunted down by his legal wife, who had trailed him from Poland.

His legal wife left in 1890. The Klosowskis moved to New Jersey in America in 1891. They then separated, each returning independently to England in 1892, and by 1893 Klosowski had met Annie Chapman, whose name he would eventually adopt, choosing George as a forename. They separated in 1895 after Annie Chapman had become pregnant.

The bodies of Chapman's two last 'wives' were exhumed in November 1892. Both corpses were remarkably well preserved, and both had large amounts of antimony in them: an effect of this strong poison is that it preserves the body for many years after death.

Chapman was charged with the murders of his three last 'wives', but was convicted only of Maud's death. On hearing of his arrest, the retired Chief Inspector Abberline, a key investigator in the Whitechapel murders (otherwise known as the Jack the Ripper Murders), complimented Godley, saying 'You've got Jack the Ripper at last!'

The moment Chapman's story filtered through the police and into the Press, Abberline suspected that Chapman and Jack the Ripper were one and the same. Jack the Ripper had knowledge of surgery, Chapman had been a surgeon, and his arrival in England (as Klosowski) coincided with the first Ripper murder, only yards away from where he lived; the murders stopped when the Klosowskis moved to America. The murders took place at weekends, showing that the murderer had a regular job, as did Chapman. Both the Ripper and Chapman led lives free of family responsibility – Miss

George Chapman. *(From a contemporary magazine)*

Baderski said that Chapman came home only in the early hours of the morning. Chapman had a formidable sex drive, as did the Ripper; Chapman was a misogynist as was the Ripper; Chapman was a known multiple killer, as was the Ripper. The description of a man seen in the company of one of the Ripper's victims before her demise seemed to fit Chapman: 'Height 5ft 6in; age 34–35, dark complexion, with moustache curled at ends' – except for his age.

There were, however, flaws in Abberline's argument. Chapman was 23 years old in 1888 and those who alleged they had seen Jack the Ripper said that the man was between 35 and 40 years old. Could the recently disembarked Polish refugee speak perfect English? The Ripper could. Serial killers normally adopt one way of despatching their victims – why would Chapman change his style? Had he?

At the same time Abberline set the record straight insofar as Dr Cream was concerned. Dr Cream had supposedly uttered the words 'I am Jack . . .' before the noose put paid to him. Cream could not have been the Ripper because he wasn't in the country when the first murder had taken place.

Chapman was tried and convicted of Maud's death on 20 March 1903. He remained impassive throughout, refused to admit his name was Klosowski and protested his innocence to the last. The jury took eleven minutes to come to a decision. His appeal was rejected and he was hanged at Wandsworth Prison on 7 April 1903.

22
FINGERPRINTING

Investigators featured in today's television crime dramas such as *Silent Witness*, *Frost* and *Morse* often depend on the assistance of the forensics department, and the fingerprint expert in particular, to help solve a case. *CSI*, the definitive series of criminal investigation through the forensics department of Las Vegas, also relies heavily on fingerprint evidence. All these programmes depend on the drama that is created by the patient search for clues to the identity of the perpetrator.

Yet the very real situation after a burglary, when the CSI (it really is called that: Crime Scene Investigation unit) has been called in, shows how important fingerprinting is in fighting crime. Burglaries are the main source of income for users and chancers. These individuals steal commodity goods that can be sold on quickly without questions asked. Electrical goods are generally taken – and most of the time the opportunists leave their fingerprints. Once lifted, fingerprints are compared against the huge databank of fingerprints held by the police.

The science of fingerprinting that we now take for granted has only come to the fore relatively recently as one of the best ways of establishing the identity of a criminal.

Fingerprinting was first consciously used as a means of identification on legal documents in China and Japan some eight hundred years ago. In Europe wax seal impressions on documents sometimes also had a finger impression, as opposed to a heraldic emblem, if the originator of the document couldn't read and had no seal – but this was somewhat later.

For centuries other, near-barbaric, forms of identification were used, such as the branding of criminals (Milady de Winter, the evil emissary of the Cardinal de Richelieu in the d'Artagnan chronicles had been branded with a fleur de lys on her shoulder – something that would hasten her eventual decapitation), or even maiming them, as the severing of a hand that had stolen, a practice still used by hard-line advocates of shariah law. The Romans employed the tattoo needle to identify and prevent desertion of home-grown and mercenary soldiers.

The first documented findings about the ridges on the hands were published by Dr Nehemiah Grew, Fellow of the College of Physicians and Fellow of the Royal Society, in 1684:

If anyone will but take the pains, with an indifferent glass to survey the palm of his hand, he may perceive . . . innumerable little ridges, of equal bigness and distance, and everywhere running parallel one with another and especially, upon the hands and first joints of the fingers and thumb. They are very regular disposed into spherical triangles and elliptics.

These ridges were also referred to by his Italian contemporary, Professor Marcello Malpighi. Indeed Malpighi is regarded as being the father of histology, the study of tissues. The lower epidermis, the 'Malpighian layer' is named after him.

The various patterns formed by the ridges on the fingers were described and named by Professor Joannes Evangelista Purkinje of Breslau University in 1823. It is to him that we owe what have become known as the standard words for each pattern. He looked at his findings from a purely scientific angle and did not associate the ridges to a means of personal identification.

The nineteenth century was a period of advances in science in all spheres. It was a century in a hurry to develop the world. The science of fingerprinting was born of the combined talents of three individuals: Dr Henry Faulds, Sir William Herschel and Sir Francis Galton.

The first to realise the individuality of each fingerprint was William Herschel (1833–1918), son and grandson of very distinguished men. He was an Assistant Joint Magistrate and Collector in Bengal and was the first to realise the validity of fingerprints for identification purposes.

Sir William Herschel (1833–1918).
(*P.G. de Loriol*)

In 1858 Herschel drew up an agreement with a local trader. The hatred engendered by the British administration in India meant that most Indians were loath to do business with the English and would quite often break their agreements, saying that the signatures on contracts were not theirs.

Herschel, realising that this was a problem, chose to use incontrovertible proof of the trader's identity to ensure that the trader did not renege. He 'dabbed his palm and fingers over with home-made oil ink and pressed the whole hand on the back of the contract'. He and the trader discussed at length the imprint of the ridges on the paper. This was the first official case when a complete hand-print was used as a means of identification.

Pleased with the result, Herschel decided to study his own hands. It was, for him, an intellectual exercise. He concluded that there were greater advantages in using fingerprints rather than the whole hand. He experimented on work colleagues and friends, whose fingers were subsequently reprinted years later. The exercise showed the immutability of the shapes of the ridges in any one individual.

In 1877 Herschel, in his capacity as a Magistrate and Collector near Calcutta, implemented his fingerprinting ideas by fingerprinting pensioners for their monthly payments, to prevent impersonation after their deaths. He eventually introduced this means of identification into the prisons, as it sometimes happened that a prisoner or his confederates hired a substitute to serve the prison sentence. Occasionally a faked death and a purchased corpse was another way to escape a prison sentence.

Heartened by his findings, on 15 August 1877 Herschel wrote a letter to the Inspector of Gaols, detailing his research and asking him to try out his new system. The letter, now known as the 'Hooghly' letter, stated that he had discovered

> a system more infallible than photography. It consists of taking a seal-like impression, in common seal-ink, of the markings on the skin of the two forefingers of the right hand . . . These marks do not change in the course of 10–15 years . . . the cogency of the evidence is admitted by everyone who takes the trouble to compare a few signatures together . . . I have taken thousands . . . and I am prepared to answer for the identity of every person whose sign-manual I can produce if I am confronted with him . . . Here is the means of identifying every man in jail with the man sentenced by the Court . . . For use in other departments especially among illiterate people . . .

After all his efforts he received only one reply, and his letter was confined to the archives.

A very controversial figure in the history of fingerprinting came to the fore in 1878 – Dr Henry Faulds (1843–1930). He was controversial because he was to dispute the credit of discovering this new science with Herschel, Galton and their disciples to the end of his life. His contribution to the new science was enormous and still remains unsung.

Faulds was a self-made and self-educated Scotsman. He was a vehement Presbyterian, short-tempered and irritable. While working as a medical missionary in Japan he discovered fingerprints on prehistoric pottery found at Omori. This intrigued him. He started extensive research on the permanence and uniqueness of fingerprints and, despite theological differences with Charles Darwin, wrote to him in 1880 about his findings, forwarding to him his classification system and a sample of the forms he had designed for recording inked impressions. Darwin was ill, but forwarded Faulds's letter and its contents to his cousin Sir Francis Galton (1822–1911), one of the greatest scientists of the age, who had an interest,

Dr Henry Faulds (1843–1930).
(P.G. de Loriol)

among many other things, in fingerprints. Galton, in turn, sent the letter on to the Anthropological Institute – but they did nothing with it because Faulds was then unknown.

In the same year Faulds published an article in the scientific journal *Nature* discussing fingerprints as a means of personal identification and the use of printer's ink to obtain fingerprints. Faulds is credited with the first fingerprint identification of a fingerprint left on an alcohol bottle.

Among the data Galton collected in his laboratory were impressions of fingers. He was able to show, like Herschel, that the fingerprint pattern remained constant as the person grew older, and he devised characteristics of the fingerprints that could be used as unique identifiers of the person, based on grouping the patterns into arches, loops and whorls.

In 1888 Galton was asked to give a lecture on the anthropometric system devised by the Frenchman Alphonse Bertillon. This system was used for identifying people by measurements of their bodily dimensions, and was widely adopted by police forces around the world following Bertillon's successful identification of a habitual criminal in 1883. The metric system, as this would be called in England, was adopted and formed the basis of a new department at Scotland Yard, the Metric Office. This was run by Dr John Garson, vice-president of the Anthropological Institute. He trained all policemen in the new system and also researched the emerging science of fingerprinting.

The anthropometric system, also known as Bertillonage, came a cropper in 1903 when a man named Will West was sentenced to prison in Kansas, USA. There was a man in the same prison with almost identical measurements, and his name was William West. Fingerprints were taken of both individuals and these were shown to be different. It later turned out that the two men were identical twins, proving the ascendancy of fingerprinting as a means of conclusive identification.

Sir Francis Galton (1822–1911). (P.G. de Loriol)

Sir Francis also decided to talk about the 'new' emerging science, fingerprinting or dactyloscopy, as it was called, in his talk. He gave the first public demonstration of the persistence of ridge characteristics. What both Galton and Herschel failed to mention was the immense contribution Dr Henry Faulds had made to this new science. They colluded in arranging that the new phenomenon would be attributed to them – the unworldly, irascible, yet more precise Scottish nobody stood no chance against these two upper-middle-class members of the English establishment.

Alphonse Bertillon (1853–1913). *(P.G. de Loriol)*

Galton was to write several books on the subject: *Finger Prints* (1893), *Blurred Finger Prints* (1893), and *Finger Print Directory* (1895). His identification system became the basis for the classification system of Sir Edward R. Henry (1850–1931), who later became Chief Commissioner of the London Metropolitan Police. The Galton-Henry system of fingerprint classification was published in June 1900, and began to be used at Scotland Yard in 1901 as an identification on criminal records. It was soon used throughout the world in criminal investigations.

The process of recognising habitual criminals in Britain was almost completely based on memory. Detectives went daily to convict parades in prison in order to memorise as many faces as possible. Warders also used this method. It was slow, but very popular among the police and warders. Edward Henry was to change this radically.

Edward Henry, later created a baronet, was Inspector-General of the Bengal police when the police force adopted the anthropometric measuring system devised by Bertillon for the identification of criminals. Henry was very interested in the potential of fingerprinting as an alternative, yet untried, method of identification and contacted and befriended Galton. In 1896 he detailed the effectiveness of Bertillon's system, showing how human error contributed to its weakness, and introduced fingerprinting as a possibly more effective system. By 1897 a resolution was passed allowing fingerprinting to be used nationwide in India.

In 1901 Edward Henry was appointed Assistant Commissioner of Scotland Yard – with this brief he set up the first official fingerprinting branch in London. One of his fingerprinting staff, DS Collins, worked on the basis that one could use fingerprints as a means of linking criminals to past crimes and as yet undetected ones. A Denmark Hill burglary on 27 June 1902 proved a turning point – the burglar left a fingerprint that had previously been recorded as belonging to a Harry Jackson. He was proved guilty.

[*Judy*, July 1, 1891

'No more the prints of hobnailed boots the bobby cute shall gauge
When forth he starts a crime to track, a criminal to cage.
No matter now how thick and deep the damning footprints fall,
He'll search for dirty finger-marks upon the tell-tale wall.
And, having found and studied these, his intellect acute
Will grasp at once who made the mark beyond the least dispute.
Once having settled this, he'll start upon the cheerful plan
Of taking everybody up—except the proper man.
So tracing crime by finger-marks may very likely come
To much resemble after all the good old rule of thumb.'

The policeman's rule of thumb

Fingerprint evidence.
(P.G. de Loriol)

The successful outcome of arrests made at the Epsom Derby in 1903, long the haunt of professional pickpockets, was used as a platform to herald the ascendancy of fingerprinting and the complete demise of the anthropometric system. Twenty-seven of the men arrested had previous convictions. Melville Macnaghten, Assistant Commissioner, long a fierce critic of the use of fingerprints, was converted. It was not until 1905, however, that the fingerprinting department got its first big break – proving guilt in a murder trial.

23
YOU'RE FINGERED!

The murder of Mr and Mrs Farrow,
Deptford, 1905

Deptford, by reason of its proximity to the river and Greenwich, had been the most important naval yard in the region and was the Royal Navy Centre for provisioning. Its slaughterhouses serviced the navy and the city. By the 1750s the Thames was silting up badly and Deptford finally closed its docks in 1869. The victualling yard, however, continued until 1961, when it closed. The world's largest electricity generating plant, built in 1897, provided a tenuous living for the inhabitants of one of London's poorest suburbs.

Deptford's demise as a thriving commercial centre was not sudden; its prolonged death was painful, changing its once thriving, although filthy, service industries into urban decay. Some streets were so dangerous that even the local bobby refused to patrol them.

The nineteenth century saw the advent of the railways, the railway terminus at the end of the High Street, and the continuing existence of the small shopkeeper. One such shopkeeper was Mr George Chapman. He was the owner of two oil and colour stores (paint shops), one in Greenwich and one,

Deptford High Street.
(P.G. de Loriol)

91

a squat, two-storeyed building at 34 High Street, Deptford. Thomas Farrow, a man in his seventies, was the manager. Both he and his 65-year-old wife lived above the little shop. Their 16-year-old assistant, William Jones, generally arrived at work for 7.30 a.m. to find the door already opened for business, as Mr Farrow always opened early to catch the early morning trade.

The morning of Monday 27 March 1905 was different. It was banking day, when the previous week's takings were taken to the bank. William Jones arrived at 8.35 a.m. to find the door of the shop locked. He rang the bell but no one answered. He looked through the letter box in the door, and saw that a chair was knocked over in the Farrows' parlour. He ran to get help from Louis Kidman, the assistant of Mr Chapman's other shop, and the two of them clambered over the dividing wall of the next-door premises. They found the scullery door open and, next to the upturned chair, the lifeless body of Mr Farrow in a pool of blood.

Sergeant Albert Atkinson was quick to arrive. He climbed the stairs and found the badly beaten Mrs Farrow still clinging to life. A doctor, Dr Burnie, was called. He and the Blackheath constabulary arrived at 9.45 a.m., followed by Melville Macnaghten, Assistant Commissioner of Scotland Yard, head of CID Chief Inspector Frederick Fox, a homicide detective and two photographers at 11.30 a.m.

The scene that greeted them, apart from the crowd of onlookers, was one of broken furniture and blood. Little could be pieced together. Obviously Farrow had let the intruder or intruders in. He had been clobbered on the head from behind. Farrow had tried to stop the intruder(s) from climbing the stairs and had been hit even harder on the head. His wife had also been hit and the contents of the cashbox under the bed had been emptied. The getaway was during the morning rush hour, the criminal(s) melting into the crowd. The police had little to go on until Macnaghten noticed that the tray of the cashbox bore a smudgy fingerprint. Carefully he wrapped it up in a handkerchief and had it sent to Detective Inspector Collins, deputy head of the Fingerprint Branch. Here was something to go on; there was little likelihood that Mrs Farrow would recover – she died four days later. The unusually clear thumbprint had no match among the 80,000 fingerprints on record, but if a suspect could be found they would see whether the thumbprint could be identified. Now for the hard work . . . seeing whether anyone recalled anything from the early hours of the morning.

Fox started a house-to-house investigation. An Ethel Stanton recalled seeing two young men running up the High Street when the milkman did his round – the milkman, Henry Jennings, had also seen the two running men, one of them wearing a brown overcoat and brown shoes, the other sporting a black moustache and wearing a blue suit, black boots and a bowler hat. Another detective overheard a discussion of the murder in a Deptford pub and heard that the Stratton brothers (already known to the police) might well have been

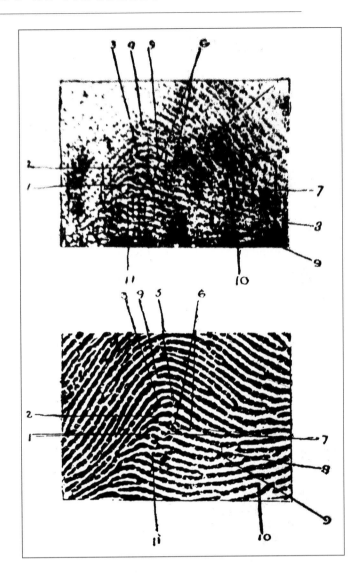

Alfred Stratton's fingerprints.
(P.G. de Loriol)

capable of it. The Stratton brothers, in their early twenties, were pimps. Fox, furthermore, discovered that Albert Stratton had taken lodgings in Knott Street and that his landlady, while cleaning his room, had discovered black stocking masks. Fox also found out that Alfred Stratton had a much-beaten girlfriend who had told the police enough to warrant an arrest – namely, that he had been out on the Sunday night, and on his return had warned her that if she were ever questioned he had spent the night with her and left her after 9 o'clock in the morning. She had also said that he had dyed his brown shoes black and had 'lost' his brown overcoat. Both brothers, large and brutish, were eventually arrested the following week and brought to the Tower Bridge police station.

The evidence Fox had garnered was not enough to secure an indictment, but Macnaghten needed to have them fingerprinted. An old police magistrate was not impressed by Fox's argument, particularly when it involved the gossip of a landlady and the ranting of a loose woman. He did, however, agree to the men's being held for a week and fingerprinted. He was sufficiently interested in this new phenomenon of 'dactyloscopy' to try it out.

Detective Superintendent Collins fingerprinted the two men and Macnaghten later recorded that he had 'returned to the office in the forenoon, and shall never forget the dramatic entry made into my room by the expert an hour or two later . . . "I have found out that the mark on the cash-box tray is in exact correspondence with the print of the thumb of the elder prisoner."' Alfred Stratton was their man! Edward Henry, now Police Commissioner of London, was immediately informed. Henry contacted Richard Muir, the Crown Prosecutor: this would be the trial that would dramatically show the importance of fingerprints.

Richard Muir took a lesson in fingerprinting, and also discovered that Ethel Stanton was prepared to swear that Alfred Stratton was one of the two running men, although the milkman who had seen two men running could not identify them. The only tangible evidence was the thumbprint. He would have to convince the jury to accept the fingerprint as evidence.

The brothers appeared in the dock at the Old Bailey on 5 May. Judge Channell, completely ignorant of dactyloscopy, presided. The two barristers for the defence were Curtis Bennett and Harold Morris; their experts were Dr Garson and the renowned Dr Faulds. Faulds had previously stated that proof of the individuality of a single print could not be used as prima facie evidence for sending a man to the block. Yet if Muir could do so, he would send the defendants to the gallows. Muir presented his case, listening to the witnesses, what they saw and heard, the movements of the brothers, their way of life, the execution of their plan, and the callous and brutal way they disposed of people. Each witness was cross-examined very effectively by the defence. Finally Muir presented the cashbox tray, a blown-up picture of the smudgy print and one of Alfred Stratton's, pointing out that the fingerprints were identical on at least eleven counts. He had members of the jury have their prints taken to reinforce his argument, and successfully identified each one despite 'discrepancies' pointed out by the defence.

Finally the defence called Dr Garson – a great mistake, as when cross-examined by Muir the latter showed a letter, written to him by Dr Garson, offering his services as a fingerprint expert, before he offered his expertise to the defence. It showed that Garson was, according to the judge, 'a completely untrustworthy witness'. The judge cautiously advised the jury that the fingerprint evidence should be regarded as valid evidence, but that their conclusion must not solely be based on the fingerprint. Two hours later the jury returned a verdict of guilty. The brothers were condemned to hang.

Albert and Alfred Stratton. *(P.G. de Loriol, from* London Stations, *1905)*

The verdict undoubtedly showed Richard Muir's talents and it also showed extraordinary luck in discrediting a noted scientist. It paved the way for the use of fingerprinting in criminal trials worldwide.

<h1>24</h1>

WHEN YOU GO DOWN TO THE WOODS . . .

*The murder of Leon Beron,
Clapham, 1911*

Clapham Common has attracted quite a lot of adverse media publicity in the last few years. The publicity has mainly centred on the 'woods' to the west of the Common, bounded by The Avenue.

It was here, just before 8 a.m. on New Year's Day 1911, that PC Joseph Mumford of the West Division was patrolling his beat, on the path from the bandstand to the northern perimeter of the woods. In those days the path had an iron railing on the right-hand side.

North-west Path, Clapham Common. *(P.G. de Loriol)*

The 'Woods' where the body was found. *(P.G. de Loriol)*

Halfway past the woods he noticed blood on the path by the iron railing. His eyes strayed to the other side of the path, noting that the flattened grass looked as if a body had been dragged into the undergrowth. It had. He found the body of a man, encased in a large black coat, under a bush, his face covered by a handkerchief, and far enough away from the path lights for it to remain unnoticed 'till the morning'.

He rushed back to Cavendish Road police station and called for assistance. The man had been killed from blows to the head. There were also two large 'S'-shaped cuts on his cheeks and stab wounds to his chest.

The police quickly established that the deceased was a 47-year-old Russian Jew called Leon Beron. He had been in the country for the last five years. He lived at 133 Jubilee Street in Whitechapel and owned nine properties, from which he collected rents. He never banked the rents, but kept a large amount of cash on his person, as well as a gold watch with a chain and a £5 gold coin attached to it. Needless to say, neither the money nor the watch was on the body. He also seemed to be a 'fence' in a minor kind of way. The police also discovered that he seemed to spend most of his time at a Jewish restaurant, Snellwars, close to his home. Its regular patrons all knew that he carried a large amount of money on him at all times. So what had the deceased been doing on Clapham Common?

The body of Leon Beron. *(P.G. de Loriol, from* Police News*)*

Further inquiries led to a cabman telling the police that he had driven two men, one of whom was Beron, to Lavender Gardens. The other man had paid him the fare on arrival, at about 2.40 a.m. The police also established that a Steinie Morrison (aka Morris Stein or Moses Tagger) had befriended the deceased a few weeks before and had been seen leaving Snellwars with him on the night before the murder. Furthermore, this Steinie Morrison seemed flush with money shortly after the murder.

On 8 January Steinie Morrison, an ex-convict, was arrested. Another cabman identified him as being the fare he had picked up at Clapham Cross in the early hours of the morning and driven to Kennington. Yet another cabman had taken him and another man from Kennington to Finsbury Park.

Morrison was taken to Leman Street police station, where he stated that 'I understand that I am detained here on a very serious charge – murder, I am told.' This would lead to some controversy in the trial, as it appeared that no one had yet told him of the charge – so he must be guilty. It transpired that one of the arresting officers had told him.

The trial at the Old Bailey was set for Monday 6 March 1911. It could not be proved directly that Steinie Morrison had murdered Leon Beron, but

einie Morrison.
G. de Loriol, from
lice News)

he had left a long parcel at the restaurant on 31 December, claiming it was a flute – but it was far too heavy. It was an iron bar. He had retrieved it when he had left with Beron. His alibis for that night did not hold up. He knew Clapham Common fairly well, as he had worked for Pithey's Bakery at 213 Lavender Hill until the local police discovered he had form and told him to leave. He was flush with money after the murder. He had been recognised by the cabbies, although neither of them attempted to see the police until at least 9 January. He also had a criminal history and usually carried a gun. Beron knew the Common, as his elderly father lived in a home down Nightingale Lane. Both Beron's brothers knew the defendant by sight.

Illustration from Police News.
(P.G. de Loriol)

The trial was interesting from a legal point of view because it illustrated the workings of the Criminal Evidence Act, 1898, allowing the prisoner to give evidence on his own behalf. Attempts by the defence to prove that the strange 'S'-shaped carvings on Beron's face were the marks of secret societies or even organised gangs were quashed.

The outcome of the trial rested not on absolute proof, nor on circumstantial evidence, but on the good sense of the jury. Most of the witnesses' statements were proved false, apart from those of the cabmen. The prisoner, however, was a tall, good-looking man and was quite candid about his previous offences. He also answered all questions to the best of his ability – all these positive aspects showed him up as a pleasant and personable man. The judge had to sum up a difficult situation. He tried to circumvent the minefield of contradictions by suggesting to the jury that if there were any reasonable doubt as to the prisoner's guilt they must act accordingly.

The jury returned a 'guilty' verdict on 15 March. Despite the case going to the Court of Appeal, the judges decided that the case stood. A petition was then presented to the Home Secretary, Winston Churchill. He commuted the sentence to penal servitude. Morrison died in Parkhurst Prison on 24 January 1921, claiming his innocence to the end.

25

THE BIRDHURST RISE MYSTERY

The poisoning of Edmund Duff, Vera and Violet Sidney, Croydon, 1928–9

In 1928 Croydon was a thriving Surrey town. The residents of South Croydon, the Coombe Lane area, were some of the more affluent of the borough. It was here that the Sidney and Duff families lived in close proximity to each other. Violet Sidney, the 70-year-old matriarch, lived with her daughter Vera, a 40-year-old spinster, at 29 Birdhurst Rise, a comfortably large Victorian house. Violet's other daughter Grace, 41, lived some five minutes away at 16 South Park Hill Road, with her husband Edmund Creighton Duff, some seventeen years her senior, and her five children; while son Tom Sidney lived with his American wife Margaret at 6 South Park Hill Road. It was a close-knit family, and the extended family visited each other regularly.

The white car stands in front of what was 6 South Park Hill Road. (*G. de Loriol*)

No. 6 South Park Hill Road, residence of Tom Sidney. *(P.G. de Loriol)*

Violet Sidney was a rare creature in the post-Victorian era: she was a divorcee. Her husband had left her after seven years of marriage. Nevertheless, she made the most of her failed marriage and surrounded herself with her family. Her ex-husband had come back into his children's lives in 1904 and had introduced Grace to a colleague from his old Indian days, Edmund Duff. Despite the disparity in their ages, Grace had married Edmund, and for the most part lived a contented life, although her husband had a relatively menial job and they were always short of money.

Edmund Duff was an unusually fit man for his age, although on the morning that he took a week's leave from his job – as a clerk with a firm of paper manufacturers – to go fishing at an old pal's in the New Forest, he visited one of the family's physicians, Dr Binning, for a prescription to relieve diarrhoea and stomach pains. Grace saw him off from South Croydon station. It was Monday 23 April 1928.

Edmund spent the whole of the next day fishing, hatless in the hot sun. On the 25th he felt slightly sick and decided not to go fishing. His host thought it might be a return of the malaria Edmund had suffered while in Nigeria.

On the morning of the 26th Edmund felt much better. He and his host had lunch together and he returned home. On his return he complained that he felt feverish. Grace called the family doctor, Robert Elwell. Edmund was brought his supper at around 7 p.m., ate only a little, but drank his customary screw-cap bottle of beer. Dr Elwell arrived shortly after 8 p.m., checked the patient's temperature – only 99°F – and prescribed aspirin, quinine and rest.

It was a good two hours before they went to bed. Walking up the stairs to his bedroom (they had separate bedrooms), Edmund felt sick and rushed to the bathroom, vomiting. Later, in the small hours of the night, Grace heard him walking about his bedroom. In the morning he tried to drink some liquids, but this made him sick – this time he also had diarrhoea. Grace called Elwell at 9.30 a.m., and again at 11 o'clock, as her husband's diarrhoea and vomiting wouldn't stop. Dr Binning, Elwell's partner, arrived at the house at about noon, examined Edmund and suggested that he try small doses of calomel.

Edmund Creighton Duff. *(P.G. de Loriol, courtesy Croydon Local History)*

Edmund's condition deteriorated. He was sweating and shivering with cold; cramps hit his feet, stomach and back. Dr Elwell called in later, not unduly worried, but mystified by the continual vomiting – it was as though Duff's body was trying to expel a foreign object. Edmund's condition worsened and by the evening the doctors thought he might be suffering from ptomaine poisoning. They also realised that his condition might be fatal. At one point he screamed out that he couldn't breathe. The devoted Grace called the doctors once again. Edmund was injected with digitalis, strychnine and pituitrin, but all to no avail. He died just after 11 p.m., twenty-seven hours after his initial nausea. His wife seemed so distressed that the two doctors continued to give Edmund artificial respiration for a good twenty minutes after he had died.

The cause of death was unknown. There had to be a post-mortem examination, then a coroner's inquest. A month later the pathologist who had performed the post-mortem, Dr Robert Brontë, declared that he was satisfied that it was a normal death, due to degeneration of the heart muscle (chronic myocarditis), and the vomiting was caused by a heart attack. He even stated that 'one can quite exclude the possibility of poisoning'. Edmund Duff was buried in Queen's Road cemetery. Grace was inconsolable. She felt the house in South Park Hill held too many bad memories and moved, with her children, to 59 Birdhurst Rise.

Vera Sidney was a masseuse, enjoyed life to the full, was a member of the local golf club and played bridge. She also had a private income and a Citroën car. Just a month short of her forty-first birthday, in January 1929, she started feeling tired and listless; then, after several weeks of this malaise, she started to have bouts of vomiting.

Sunday 10 February was another trying day for her. She felt particularly ill and stayed home all day. During Grace's visit that evening Vera told her she was feeling particularly unwell. Vera's solution to her problem was to go for a brisk walk and play bridge with friends the next day. But by the time she returned home she felt rotten again. She and the cook, Mrs Noakes, had some soup for supper, as did the family cat. Violet did not.

Soon after supper both Mrs Noakes and Vera were violently sick. Both of them vomited during the night and the cook noticed, in the morning, that the cat had also been sick on the kitchen floor. Vera was too weak to get up, but managed to dress for tea because Grace was coming.

Vera felt much better on Wednesday 13th. She ate breakfast and went out, returning to meet her visiting aunt, Mrs Gwendoline Greenwell of Newcastle-upon-Tyne, for a pre-arranged lunch. Noakes made a soup, and cooked chicken, vegetables and a custard pudding. Grace could not join them as she was seeing to the children's lunch. Vera and her aunt had some soup, although her aunt only had a few spoonfuls. Both were sick and diarrhoeic immediately after the meal. Vera was convinced that it was the soup. The aunt returned to London and spent six days recovering.

Vera, meanwhile, was very ill. Grace called Dr Elwell. He arrived at 9 p.m. At midnight he gave Vera a morphine injection and stayed on until 2.30 a.m.

Both Dr Elwell and Dr Binning returned the next day, staying the whole day. They consulted a specialist in gastro-intestinal diseases, Dr Charles Bolton. He opined that Vera was suffering from gastro-intestinal influenza. Vera then had pains in her feet and stomach. She went into a stupor and eventually died, just after midnight on Friday 15 February 1929. Drs Binning and Elwell both agreed on the cause of death and signed the death certificate accordingly – she had died of gastro-intestinal disease. She too was buried in Queen's Road cemetery.

The matriarch, Violet Sidney, was appalled by the loss of her doting daughter. They had been together for so many years. Edmund's death had been a jolt, but she had never really approved of Edmund Duff – he was too old and a friend of her ex-husband. She had always favoured the handsome and single Dr Elwell. Both Grace and Tom thought Violet would just give up the ghost.

The redoubtable 70-year-old soldiered on. Dr Elwell visited her on a daily basis, prescribing her Metatone and Phylosan tablets. By Tuesday 5 March her blood pressure had considerably improved and her pulse was much stronger. Dr Elwell was pleased with her improvement.

Violet had lunch but felt ill halfway through the pudding. Grace called round with some shopping her mother had asked for, and later she said that 'her face was absolutely deathly white, just as if she were dead'. Violet told Grace that she thought she had been poisoned because her last dose of Metatone had been very strong and tasted gritty. Mrs Noakes thought it was the medicine the doctor had been prescribing. Grace called the doctor, but before Dr Binning could arrive Violet had vomited and had diarrhoea. Violet told him that she had been poisoned, and while Grace put her mother to bed Dr Binning noticed some grainy sediment in the Metatone bottle.

Tom Sidney visited his mother during the afternoon. His mother repeated her fears, but Dr Elwell discounted the poison theory when he arrived. He thought she might well have caught food poisoning. Dr Binning, meanwhile, had checked the constituents of the Metatone with the local chemist. The chemist assured him that the only poison in it was 1/96 part of a grain of strychnine, far short of a fatal dose.

Violet seemed to get better during the afternoon, but suffered a relapse at about 4 p.m. Dr Elwell called in a nurse and a specialist, Dr Frederic Poynton. Dr Poynton thought Violet had succumbed to either copper poison or poisoning by ptomaine. He couldn't come to a firm conclusion, although he would later say that her death was due to food poisoning.

The doctors couldn't help her. Violet died at 7.30 p.m., with Elwell and Binning in attendance. This time, however, they couldn't come to any conclusion and couldn't issue a death certificate. Dr Henry Beecher Jackson, Croydon coroner, ordered a post-mortem and Dr Brontë carried it out. He had the major organs sent for analysis.

The police were alerted. Detective Inspectors Fred Hedges and Reg Morrish of the Croydon CID arrived at 29 Birdhurst Rise with Tom Sidney. They searched the premises and removed some bottles. They then went to Dr Binning to collect the Metatone.

The inquest on Violet's death opened two days later, but it was adjourned until 4

This modern block stands on the site of 29 Birdhurst Rise. (*P.G. de Loriol*)

No. 33 Birdhurst Rise is identical to No. 29.
(P.G. de Loriol)

April. Violet Sidney was buried at Queen's Road cemetery next to her daughter.

It was only now that the Press scented a possible story. On 19 March the police visited the Sidney family graves, armed with exhumation orders for the bodies of Vera and Violet Sidney. They had by now amassed much new evidence. Arsenic had been found in the residue of Violet's medicine bottle and her organs were also riddled with arsenic.

Sir Bernard Spilsbury, the honorary pathologist to the Home Office, performed the post-mortem. He came to the conclusion that Vera had died of arsenical poisoning. Vera and Violet were reburied on 25 March 1929. It was then considered expedient that Edmund Duff be exhumed. This was done seven weeks later, on 18 May.

Spilsbury examined the grave and noted that the body was in a remarkable state of preservation – a typical effect of arsenic poisoning. Grace Duff had already attended her mother's and sister's inquests. She would have to go through yet another one. The *Daily Express* reported that she said 'It was dreadful for me to have the body of my husband exhumed. It seemed such a desecration; worse than the first burial. But I am glad they did it if it will help to discover the truth. We were such a united family, splendid friends.'

The results warranted a second inquest on Edmund Duff's death. This started on 5 July 1929. The inquests on Violet and Vera Sidney were nearly finished. The duration of the collected inquests spanned five months and in all three cases Tom and Grace were represented by the barrister Richard Fearnley-Whittingstall.

Violet's inquest ruled that her death was caused by acute arsenical poisoning. Arsenic had been found in both the Metatone bottle and the wine glass from which she had drunk the Metatone. But had she committed suicide, had arsenic found its way into her medicine by accident, had arsenic got there through the criminal negligence of someone else, or had she been murdered? Dr Beecher Jackson, the Coroner, asked the jury to consider who might have committed such a heinous crime. Was it the demure, quiet and softly spoken Grace, who had never shown any ill-feeling towards her mother; or was it

Tom Sidney, a garrulous man who had not taken the inquest too seriously and whose statements seemed to be only partly truthful? The jury returned a verdict of 'acute poisoning by arsenic'. They could not establish whether it was suicide or murder.

Vera's inquest followed the same path and produced the same results. Sir Bernard Spilsbury opined that it was the soup. Mrs Noakes made a curious and serious allegation against Tom Sidney, as did Detective Inspector Reg Morrish. Tom's propensity for making damaging statements was seriously harming his reputation.

Dr Beecher Jackson once again directed the jury and exonerated the quiet and composed Grace, saying that she and her sister were on the best of terms. He also did his best for Tom, saying that he was on very good terms with the whole of the extended family. The jury returned a verdict of 'murdered by arsenical poisoning wilfully administered by person or persons unknown'.

The last inquest, and the second inquest on Edmund Duff, proved humiliating for Dr Brontë. His original findings were rebutted. He may have mixed up Edmund's organs with another autopsy, although he denied this. His change of mind amounted to an apology, as he categorically stated that all Edmund Duff's organs showed large doses of strychnine. He told the inquest that Sir Bernard Spilsbury's analysis had changed his mind.

Grace Duff thought the arsenic was in a whisky flask her husband had taken with him on his fishing trip, while Sir Bernard thought it was more likely to have been in the beer he had when he returned home. Tom Sidney highlighted a less flattering side to Grace when he related an altercation between her and her husband before Edmund had gone fishing – possibly in an attempt to counter the adverse opinion the inquest had of him.

The Coroner concluded that there was 'no evidence which singles out any one member of the family as the poisoner'. The jury ascribed his death as 'murdered by some person or persons unknown'. The case remains unresolved to this day.

The killer owed his or her anonymity to professional incompetence. Had the original post-mortem on Edmund Duff detected arsenic, the killer would probably never have continued. Because of the original findings the police were unable to investigate from the start. Dr Henry Beecher Jackson decided to hold three separate inquests for the three bodies. This meant three different juries, contrary to the DPP's instructions. They had expressly asked that they be held concurrently, with one jury. This would have given the opportunity for one jury to see the similarities and for the coroner to ask more questions.

The coroner was particularly soft on Grace Duff. She was the consummate actress, dressing as a grieving widow should, speaking in low and clear tones and playing to the audience. She stood to benefit from quite a substantial inheritance from the three deaths – and she needed the money. Tom Sidney was a brash, professional (but failed) actor/musician and entertainer. He and his young American wife had come back to England because he couldn't provide for her and their child – he was always short of money.

The police had discounted Mrs Noakes, but thought there was something to Tom's comment that Dr Elwell and Grace Duff were more than good friends. When Vera and Violet died another, somewhat more sinister, side to Grace emerged. She had seemed more excited than sorrowful, and shouted out to a neighbour that the police thought she had murdered her husband. Another anecdote concerned an elderly lodger of the Duffs, Miss Kelvey. She was frightened of Grace and, on her deathbed, told Grace that she was wicked. Grace had laughed. Miss Kelvey was 76 when she died, but there has been quite a lot of controversy over her death – maybe, if the body had been exhumed, arsenic might have been found?

Detective Inspector Hedges, who had led the investigation, was quite sure, for the most part, that Tom was the culprit. He then changed his mind after weeks of watching Grace on the witness stand. He wrote in his notebook,

> there is no doubt in my mind that she was secretly in love with Dr Elwell. I believe that she poisoned her husband, perhaps hoping that Elwell would marry her . . . I think she killed Vera thinking she would stand a better chance of catching Dr Elwell if she had more money of her own. She murdered her mother in order to acquire even more money. There is something cold and sinister about that woman.

Her counsel, Richard Whittington-Egan, also strongly suspected she was the poisoner.

Grace was a pretty and vivacious woman. She had married a man somewhat older, who was highly sexed and regularly made her pregnant – something she wasn't too happy about. She and Elwell were certainly very friendly, and the old adage 'cherchez la femme' may well be true in this case.

26

THE BAPTIST CHURCH
MURDER

The murder of Rachel Dubinski,
Kennington, 1941

The Second World War wreaked untold havoc among the population of London. Flying bombs targeted and wrecked many supply lines in the capital, railways, depots and public buildings. While the majority of the population tried to muddle through, some more opportunistic individuals made money on the black market, dealt in stolen goods, and thieved and murdered in the hopes that their misdemeanours would never be discovered or would be mistaken for casualties in the rubble of the bombings.

The following case proved fundamental to the development of forensic dentistry. St Oswald's Place Baptist Church, just off Kennington Lane (SE11) had been severely bomb-damaged during Luftwaffe raids between October 1940 and March 1941. Benjamin Marshall, a demolition worker, was sifting through the rubble of the church on 7 July 1942. He prised up a large stone slab and discovered the curiously well-preserved body of a female. His statement said it all: 'I stood the stone on its edge. Underneath I saw some human remains. The head was nearest the steps. I noticed some of the bones were missing. I noticed some white substance round the bones.'

It was at first assumed that the body was either that of a bomb victim or a corpse from the old burial ground. The burial ground had not been used for fifty years. Protocol had to be observed. The police were called in and Dr Keith Simpson, a pathologist, was also summoned.

Dr Simpson found something curious. The body was not, as had previously been thought, an old relic of the graveyard. He found it strange that a bomb victim should neatly bury itself under a stone slab, or even jump into a fire, covered in quicklime. Bomb victims did not have neatly severed limbs or head. Someone had obviously tried to disguise the corpse's identity.

Simpson had the body taken to Southwark mortuary. There he established that the time of death was between twelve and fifteen months before. The subject was female, in her forties, had dark greying hair, was 5ft 1in tall and suffered from a fibroid tumour. A blood clot in the throat seemed to indicate that the woman had been strangled. Simpson also went back to the place where the body had been found and discovered that the ground was covered with quicklime – this had obviously been used to stop the smell of decay, but it had also stopped the work of maggots and preserved the body.

This was definitely murder. The police archives were trawled through. A Mrs Rachel Dobkin, answering the basic description, had been reported missing about a year before. Her handbag had been discovered in Guildford and handed over to her family. Her sister, Polly Dubinski, had found the business card of a spiritualist medium in the bag, had contacted him, and when she had said she was Ray's sister, the medium had told her that her sister had been strangled and hit on the head and that Polly would never see her again.

Polly had contacted the police on 12 April 1941, but they'd had no luck. On the 14th a small fire broke out in the ruins of the Baptist church. Somewhat strange, as there had been no air raids . . . When the fire brigade arrived a Mr Dobkin was trying to put it out. He explained that the fire had started at 1.30 a.m. but as it wasn't big enough to cause too much concern he had not called the authorities. He was interviewed three times in all, but the exigencies of war meant that the matter was dropped.

Dr Simpson set to work to try to determine the identity of the victim. Part of the lower jaw was missing, but the upper jaw showed that there had been extensive work done on the teeth. Polly Dubinski confirmed that Rachel had a dentist, a Dr Kopkin. Dr Kopkin had kept records of the work done on Mrs Dobkin. A chart of her upper jaw matched exactly with that of the victim. Her sister confirmed that Rachel had indeed suffered from a fibroid tumour. The head of the Photography Department at Guy's Hospital superimposed a photograph of the skull on a photograph of Rachel Dobkin. This was a technique that had first been used six years earlier in a case in Scotland (the Buck Ruxton case). The fit was perfect.

It transpired that Rachel had been married – through a matchmaker, in the traditional Jewish fashion – to Harry Dobkin in 1920. Theirs had been a mismatched pairing. They had stayed together for six weeks and then divorced. Unfortunately for Harry, Rachel gave birth to a son and demanded maintenance for him for the next twenty years.

The police searched for Dobkin and found him in Dalston. He was arrested on 26 August 1942. They established that he had been a fire-watcher at a firm of solicitors next to the church at about the time of his wife's death. He had paid his ex-wife's maintenance grudgingly and had even defaulted on payments, for which he had spent some time in prison. He had also been summonsed four times for assault. In short, he was a very bitter man, who resented having to pay for a mistake committed some twenty years earlier.

Harry Dobkin. *(P.G. de Loriol, from Police News)*

Dobkin was escorted to the church, where, despite protestations of never having been there, he was recognised by a boy who had seen him several times in the crypt. A search of his premises revealed some quicklime, identical to that discovered at the Baptist church. He continued to swear that the body was not that of his wife.

His trial started on 17 November 1942 at the Old Bailey. Mr Justice Wrottesley presided. Dobkin's defence lawyer vainly tried to challenge the process of identification, but the prosecution had made too good a case. Dobkin's appearance in the witness box did not impress the jury. It took twenty minutes to reach a decision – guilty. The judge had also decided, and said as much: 'After a most patient hearing the jury has come to what I think is the right conclusion on this matter.'

Dobkin confessed to his wife's murder before the execution. He had met her in Kingsland Road, Shoreditch, near his home in Navarino Road, Dalston. He had wined and dined her, then strangled her. He hid her body in his flat and then made some very serious mistakes. First he cut off the head at the neck, the arms at the elbows, and the legs at the knees. Then he put quicklime all over the corpse, thinking as most people do that quicklime dissolves bodies. It doesn't, especially when it is mixed with water. It burns the skin, but the intense heat created by the chemical reaction dries out the body and 'mummifies' it. He then interred the body in the bombed-out Baptist church and tried to burn it beyond recognition – hence the small fire at the church on 14 April 1941.

Harry Dobkin was hanged at Wandsworth Prison on 7 January 1943.

27

LET HIM HAVE IT, CHRIS!

The murder of PC Miles, Croydon, 1952

This case has supplied the press with ample material for more than sixty years, and is one of the most contentious cases in the history of the modern British judicial system.

Post-war Britain was a mess. Huge expenses during the war, the destruction of buildings and public services by the enemy, and returning soldiers with no civilian jobs created a malaise that took Britain a long time to overcome. London was a prime example. The rise in crime, especially among the youth, spiralled out of control. Official figures showed that criminal activity had risen 250 per cent since the beginning of the war. The Croydon murder case was to highlight this in more ways than one.

In 1952 the 16-year-old Chris Craig was a bored but lively teenager. He had been in trouble for quite some years and had long harboured the ambition to be a criminal. He lived in a comfortable house and had six siblings in responsible jobs and one in prison. Nevin, the black sheep of the family, was a small-time crook who had finally been caught, much to the chagrin of his parents, and sent to prison on 31 October 1952, despite pleading that he had never been involved in a failed armed robbery. The father, an ex-captain in the military, held a responsible job in town. Nevin was Chris's idol – it came as quite a jolt to find that he had disappeared from his life. Chris had always carried a gun, even through school. It was his prop, much as cigarettes are props for other teenagers. He was semi-literate, but was an excellent athlete.

Derek Bentley was 19. He was a tall, strong youth from a completely different background. His family had moved from the inner London slums to the Norbury area. Despite his physique and his carefree approach to the world, Derek had marked disadvantages; he had epilepsy, had a mental age of 11 and suffered from headaches. He had some form, then worked successfully for a removals firm but had hurt his back. He had then worked for Croydon

hris Craig. *(P.G. de Loriol, courtesy of Croydon
ocal History)*

Derek Bentley. *(P.G. de Loriol, courtesy of Croydon
Local History)*

Borough Council. At school, where they met, the two boys were inseparable.
Although Bentley left soon after they met they renewed their friendship in
1951, when he returned from an approved school. He was anti-guns and
always shied away from any 'job' that involved a gun.

The Bentley parents actively discouraged the two adolescents from seeing
each other – they realised they were 'trouble' as a team. They even begged the
police to do something about it, but to no avail. Chris, though, knew how to
get around the problem, and on that fateful night of 2 November 1952 he
arranged for two friends to ask the Bentleys whether their son could come out
with them. It worked.

The two, dressed in clothes that made them look a little older, took a bus to
Croydon on that wet night. Their object was to 'do' a butcher's premises on
Tamworth Road, but the shop was still occupied. They turned their attention
to the confectionery warehouse of Barlow & Parker.

At about 9.15 p.m. Detective Frederick Fairfax of the Croydon police
received a message from a Mr Ware. Two people had broken into the premises
of a warehouse opposite his house. Fairfax collected a few officers and they

sped to the scene. A call went out to a patrol car driven by 42-year-old PC Sidney Miles. His colleague, PC James McDonald, took the call. He turned the car round on London Road and sped to the scene of the crime.

Fairfax and his colleague Norman Harrison were the first to arrive. He spoke to Mrs Ware and clambered into the alleyway that ran the whole length of the warehouse. McDonald arrived shortly afterwards, joining Fairfax in the alleyway. Fairfax then clambered up the first drainpipe that led to a flat roof.

The flat roof had four 6ft skylights. Behind them there was the head of a lift shaft, a good 11ft tall, and 80ft away from the lift shaft was the head of a staircase. Fairfax saw two moving shadows between the roof-lights and the head of the lift shaft.

'I'm a police officer. Come out from behind the stack.'

'If you want us fucking well come out and get us,' came the reply. Fairfax rushed out to the lift-head and got hold of Bentley. He dragged Bentley round it, trying to get Craig. They came face to face. Bentley pulled himself free and shouted 'let him have it, Chris!' Craig pulled a pistol from his pocket and fired, hitting Fairfax in the shoulder. Fairfax fell to the ground and then groggily got to his feet, finding himself between Bentley and Craig.

Meanwhile, the gunshot had galvanised the police below. The night was dark and cloudy, and the police could only communicate by shouting. Fairfax knocked Bentley to the ground, dragged him in front of himself as cover, and retreated as far as he could from Craig. He then frisked Bentley, finding only a knuckleduster and knife. PC McDonald tried once more to scale the drainpipe and PC Harrison edged along the adjoining roof towards Craig.

The streets below were now swarming with fire engines, ambulances, police vans and squad cars. Craig saw Harrison and shot at him. Harrison dropped, his torch falling into the gutter. He was not hurt, but he erred on the side of caution. Fairfax was now joined by McDonald and told him that the gun was a .45 Colt. Craig fired again at the retreating Harrison. The Tamworth Road battle had now lasted a full thirty minutes.

Noises in the building below confirmed to Fairfax that his colleagues had finally contacted the manager, who had opened up the premises. PC Miles was the first to reach the roof entrance. He shoved at the door but it wouldn't budge. He tried again, the door flew open and he jumped onto the roof. A shot rang out. A bullet went through his skull. He died instantly. Fairfax pulled him behind the entrance. Craig fired again at Harrison. Harrison threw what he could in retaliation: truncheon, brick and milk bottle. Craig retaliated with several shots, shouting 'I am Craig, you've just given my brother twelve years. Come on you coppers. I'm only sixteen.'

More police arrived and were sheltering behind the roof entrance. They decided to get Bentley out of the way and, using him as a shield, rushed towards the roof entrance. Bentley warned Craig that the police were taking him down.

Craig now felt alone on the roof. He was losing his cool and feeling nervous. He shouted expletives and tried to fire his gun again. It was empty. Fairfax jumped onto the roof, fired at Craig, and missed. Craig ran towards him and dived off the building. He broke his breastbone and fractured his spine and his left arm. He was handcuffed by a policeman and taken to Croydon Hospital. Bentley was taken to be questioned at Croydon police station.

This, the official prosecution version, ensured that Craig was sent to prison, while Bentley hanged.

Bentley should have been charged with armed robbery, or as an accessory to murder. He didn't possess a firearm, was technically in police custody when PC Miles was shot, and was alleged to have said the words that incriminated him beyond a measure of a doubt – 'Let him have it, Chris!' It could have meant 'shoot the man', but Bentley was afraid of guns and would never have gone out with Craig had he known he was carrying a piece. His abhorrence of guns was well known both in his family and to Craig. He most probably meant for Chris to give the gun to the policeman – if indeed he did say that. The fact that Bentley was 19 also meant that he would get the stiffer sentence.

What was also glossed over was the fact that the gun wasn't recovered until later; the bullet that killed PC Miles was also never recovered; nor was an arms expert asked for an opinion on what gun could have killed the policeman. Neither of the two lads admitted that Bentley said what the police claimed. Strangely enough, an identical phrase had been reported in an arrest some years earlier. Bentley also, despite not being handcuffed, offered no resistance and waited with the police for a good thirty minutes before the end of the affair.

Craig had sawn off the barrel of the gun – this would make it less accurate, making the likelihood of shooting a man between the eyes at some distance, in the dark, almost impossible. Who, then, could have shot?

Lord Goddard, the Lord Chief Justice, presided over the trial on Tuesday 9 December 1952. His remit, whether self-imposed or directed, was to make an example of the two. His sentence was harsh. He wanted to discourage others from doing the same, but succeeded in doing the opposite. He completely disregarded Bentley's obvious problems and the inconsistencies in the arguments of the prosecution. The debate over the bullet that had killed PC Miles was inconclusive and the bullet presented in court had no blood on it. The missing gun then turned up in the middle of the trial. Craig was given a custodial sentence at Her Majesty's Pleasure and Bentley was convicted of 'joint enterprise' on the testimony of three police officers who had heard Bentley shout the words that sent him to the gallows. He was sentenced to death.

Wandsworth Prison. *(P.G. de Loriol)*

Bentley was hanged at Wandsworth Prison on 28 January 1953. His appeal had been heard and dismissed on 13 January 1953. The victim was a police officer, and someone had to pay. Bentley did. His father led a campaign for a reprieve and 200 MPs signed a petition, but to no avail.

Bentley's father was not satisfied. He carried the torch for his son, repeatedly asking for a belated pardon. His daughter, Iris, Bentley's sister, took up the cause when her father died. Unfortunately, she died before a final judgment was made in November 1997.

On 1 April 1997 the case was re-presented to the Criminal Case Review Commission. It referred it to the Court of Appeal on 6 November 1997. The appeal was heard before the Lord Chief Justice, Lord Bingham, Lord Kennedy and Mr Justice Collins from 20 to 24 July 1998.

The Court of Appeal ruled, on 30 July 1998, that Bentley's conviction was unsafe. The Lord Chief Justice opined that, in the Court's judgment, the previous ruling by his predecessor, Lord Goddard, 'was such as to deny the appellant that fair trial which is the birthright of every British citizen'. Lord Bingham added that 'it must be a matter of profound and continuing regret that this mistrial occurred and that the defects we have found were not recognised at the same time'.

28

THE LAW OF MISRULE

The murder of Maxwell Confait, Catford, 1972

The fire brigade was called to a house in Doggett Road, Catford, SE6 at 1.21 a.m. on Saturday 22 April 1972 by Winston Goode, a West Indian and the owner of the property. Doggett Road is parallel to the railway line near Catford Bridge station. The house was on fire, but the fire had not yet reached the first floor. Station Officer Speed and two other firemen entered the house to look for any occupants – the owner said he had a lodger. The back upstairs bedroom was locked. Speed broke down the door to find the room full of smoke and the body of a man on the floor near the bed. He felt for a pulse: there was none. He then opened the window to let out the smoke and went back downstairs to help put out the fire. The police arrived after another ten minutes, followed half an hour later by the divisional police surgeon, Dr Angus Bain.

The corpse was that of a 26-year-old of mixed race. From his make-up and clothes Dr Bain surmised that the man was a homosexual. The lips were swollen and blue, and there was a mark around the neck where a cord or flex had been twisted round it to strangle the victim. It was fairly simple, yet the consequences would not be. The young man, Maxwell Confait, had died of asphyxia due to strangulation. Dr Bain refrained from taking the rectal temperature, the procedure for working out the time of death, just in case he destroyed any evidence of recent sexual activity. Rigor mortis, however, had almost completely set in. He worked out that the victim had died between 8 p.m. and 10 p.m. the previous day.

Dr James Cameron, the pathologist, arrived at 3.45 a.m. He observed that the body was cool to the touch. Rigor mortis, he opined, had only just set in. His estimation of the time of death differed. He thought the death had occurred between 7.45 p.m. and 11.45 p.m. He also avoided taking the rectal temperature.

The body was taken to Lewisham mortuary, where Dr Cameron undertook the post-mortem examination by 6.30 a.m. The police returned to search the house and discovered that the fire had been started deliberately – a petrol

Doggett Road, Catford. *(P.G. de Loriol)*

can under the stairs in the basement had been ignited. They also discovered a length of electrical flex in the dead man's room, but there was no sign of a struggle and no fingerprints. Detective Chief Superintendent Alan Jones had now been put in charge of the case. A murder room was set up at Lee Road police station.

The police first interviewed Confait's landlord. Winston Goode had broken up with his wife some two years previously, although his wife and children still occupied the ground floor. Maxwell Confait was a male prostitute, but his alter ego, Michelle, was a transvestite. He preferred to be called Michelle. Michelle and Goode had first met at the Black Bull pub in Lewisham in 1970. Goode seemed to develop an unhealthy fixation on Michelle, following him to all his haunts and even dressing up in women's clothes. Confait moved into the back room of Goode's house in February 1972, for a nominal rent. He cooked for the two of them while Goode worked on a building site. Goode said that he had been asleep in his room in the basement when he was woken by the fire. He had run upstairs to alert his family and shouted for Confait.

The police interviewed Goode's wife. She told them that she thought her husband behaved very strangely that night, almost grief-stricken. She even sent a neighbour after him when he went to phone the firemen from a call-box. The neighbour said that he was desperately trying to dial, and had to dial the number for him.

Goode was re-interviewed. Confait had told him he was thinking of leaving to live with a lover. Goode admitted that he felt pangs of jealousy, but categorically denied that he was in a relationship with Michelle. Samples of his semen and hair were taken and then, totally confused over what had happened, he was admitted to a psychiatric hospital.

On Monday 24 April several small fires broke out in the area surrounding Doggett Road: one on a rail embankment behind Doggett Road, one in a sports hut in Ladywell fields, and another, more serious one, at an abandoned house, at 1 Nelgarde Road, the next street.

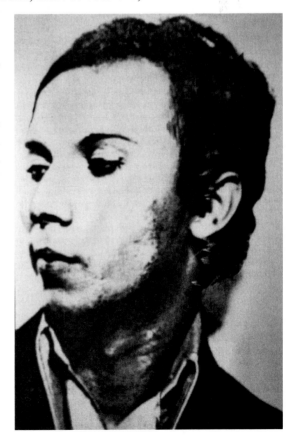

At about 5 o'clock that afternoon a policeman driving his Panda car down Nelgarde Road stopped 18-year-old Colin Lattimore. Colin was educationally subnormal and had a mental age of 8. The policeman asked him about the fires and Colin admitted to starting them. The

Maxwell Confait.
(Lewisham Local History)

119

policeman then asked him about Doggett Road, and the youth said that he had been with 15-year-old Ronnie Leighton and admitted that they had lit the fire but then put it out, leaving it smoking. The police escorted Lattimore to Leighton's house on Doggett Road, where they also asked 14-year-old Ahmet Salih to accompany them to Lewisham police station. They then went on to Lee Road police station, where all three were questioned separately by DCS Jones and Detective Inspector Graham Stockwell.

It was during these interviews that the police made some mistakes that were to have far-reaching consequences. The interviews took place without the presence of a solicitor or a parent – the law, as it stands, states that a parent, a guardian or an adult civilian of the same sex should always be present when officers interview a child. Both Lattimore and Salih also claimed that they had been hit at Lewisham police station, while Leighton claimed he had been pushed around.

That evening all the parents were asked to witness their sons' statements, a somewhat irregular procedure. Lattimore and Leighton both admitted to having started the fire and murdering Confait. Ahmet admitted to having helped to start the fire, but to having only watched the murder. By Tuesday all three were charged with murder. DCS Jones felt very pleased with himself.

The charge of murder against Ahmet Salih was dropped in May, while the two other youths were committed for trial, based on their confessions, at Woolwich Magistrates' Court on 2 June 1972. Their legal representatives were quite confident of getting the boys acquitted. Both Drs Bain and Cameron re-affirmed their belief that Confait had been murdered between 6.30 and 10.30 on the Friday evening. All three boys, however, had alibis for this time.

Colin had spent the day at a remedial school he attended, and then went home for tea and spent the evening at the local youth club, returning late and watching TV with his parents, and making quite a noise in his bedroom until 12.45 a.m. Ahmet and Ronnie, meanwhile, had stayed at Ronnie's house with two girls. They then walked to a bus stop outside a cinema after 9 p.m. They had cased a shoe shop in Sangley Road and broken into it, stealing a small sum of money, and then returned to Ahmet's and watched TV until past midnight. They had then returned to the shoe shop, but had been arrested as they left it at 1.30 a.m. and escorted back home. How could they be responsible for the murder if the time of death was correct?

The three were tried at the Old Bailey on 1 November 1972. Mr Justice Chapman presided. The medical evidence was crucial and both doctors now had second thoughts. They now thought the heat of the fire, strangulation and possibly alcohol had speeded up the onset of rigor mortis and revised the time of death to possibly as late as 1 a.m. This invalidated the boys' alibis. The defence parried with Goode's peculiar behaviour, but this was thrown out by the judge, who then delivered a homily on the evils of hooliganism.

The jury retired for three and a half hours on 24 November. Colin Lattimore was found guilty of manslaughter and arson and was ordered to be detained in a mental hospital without a time limit. Ronnie Leighton was found guilty of murder and arson, as well as burglary at Sangley Road, and sentenced to life imprisonment, while Ahmet Salih was found guilty of arson and burglary at Sangley Road and sentenced to four years in a juvenile prison.

The boys' appeal was refused on 26 July 1973, but Colin's father, George, believed in his son's innocence. He lodged a complaint against the officer who had assaulted his son at Lewisham police station, but this was quashed. He then wrote to everyone who he thought might be able to help. His local MP, Mr Carol Johnson, wrote to the Home Office, but the replies were evasive: the Home Office believed that if this were a miscarriage of justice, then there were serious flaws in the judicial system and policing. The National Council for Civil Liberties, however, contacted one of the most experienced pathologists in the country, Professor Donald Teare. His opinion of the medical aspects of the case differed quite markedly from those of Bain and Cameron. He completely denied that the heat and fire had had any effect on the onset of rigor mortis and stated that death had occurred between 6.30 and 10.30 in the evening.

The General Election of February 1974 brought about changes. The new Home Office Minister, Roy Jenkins, decided to review procedures covering miscarriages of justice. The new MP for Lewisham, Christopher Price, became interested in the case. Winston Goode committed suicide, and the police were ordered to set up an inquiry. DCS Jones was also targeted for his somewhat cavalier and possibly illegal procedures in a number of cases.

Professor Keith Simpson was also commissioned to compile a report – his findings were very similar to Donald Teare's. Finally, in 1975 Roy Jenkins announced that the Confait case had been sent back to the Court of Appeal. The appeal was launched on 6 October 1975 before Lord Scarman. It became obvious that this case would be quite different, as even Lord Scarman questioned the witnesses. The fire expert in the previous trial was allowed to give more substantial evidence than he had done before. He thought the heat had not been great enough to alter the advance of rigor mortis and did not believe Goode had tried to warn Confait. Professors Donald Teare and Keith Simpson tore the medical evidence apart, and on 17 October the three, by now, young men were exonerated from any involvement in the murder of Maxwell Confait. All three were freed.

The outcome of this was that in 1977 Sir Henry Fisher, an ex-judge, was commissioned to set up an inquiry into the review of the protocol of police questioning in all its aspects. This laid down the tenets of the English Police and Criminal Evidence Act 1984, known as PACE. Lord Scarman also threw a stick into the fire by suggesting that if Maxwell Confait had not struggled, as the evidence seemed to indicate, then he must have known his killer . . . wasn't strangulation sometimes used to heighten pleasure during sex?

29

DNA

DNA is on everybody's lips, literally. Deoxyribonucleic acid is a chemical found in virtually every cell of an organism. It carries genetic information from one generation to the next and determines physical characteristics such as eye and hair colour. This information is in the form of a code or language. Every individual's DNA is unique. Half the DNA is inherited from the father and half from the mother. Each child inherits different combinations of DNA from the parents and is different from its siblings.

The beauty of DNA is that it can be extracted from any cell that contains a nucleus: blood, semen, saliva, skin, even hair samples – and only a minute sample is needed. It can be used to determine the parents or family of an individual and has recently been used to determine the descendants of an individual whose bones were found in a churchyard some 500 years ago.

DNA has also been used to trace or even prove that an individual is a criminal – this is in the realm of forensic biology and is called DNA profiling, and it has been used to great effect during the last fifteen years. The main tenet of this science is that 'every contact leaves a trace'. DNA is unique inasmuch as a DNA profile is unique within 10 million people.

The DNA process starts at the police station when an officer takes a sample of saliva and skin from the mouth of anyone suspected of, charged with, reported for or convicted of a recordable offence, using a small, grooved, plastic stick. This stick loosens and collects skin cells that contain DNA. The stick is sealed in a tube and is sent for processing.

At the laboratory a chemical is mixed with the sample. The sample is heated for up to four hours in an oven, then boiled and spun. The resulting liquid is then extracted – this contains the DNA. Part of the liquid is then amplified in a cooling and heating process, creating millions of copies of the original DNA – a bit like a biological photocopier. The amplified DNA sample is then separated into the eleven specific areas that make up the profile by running it through an electrically charged gel between two pieces of glass. These can then be viewed as coloured bands on a computer screen while the computer works out their sizes and produces a series of numbers for each area of the DNA. A sex indicator and the numbers make up an individual's DNA profile.

The series of numbers is then entered into the national DNA database by the Forensic Science Service.

Britain has the world's first and largest National Criminal Intelligence DNA Database – the NDNAD. It was set up in 1995 and now contains upwards of five million samples. It currently matches about 2,000 samples a week.

There are, however, some negative aspects to DNA profiling. Insurance companies, for instance, have been known to take a sample from a potential client so as to decide whether the client is worth the risk. Someone may not want to have a sample of hair or skin taken, and the fact that it may be taken forcibly undermines the constitutional rights of an individual as well as civil liberties. Recent DNA sampling has taken the massive step of researching the genetic link between race and violent tendencies in the Afro-Caribbean races, a somewhat contentious issue.

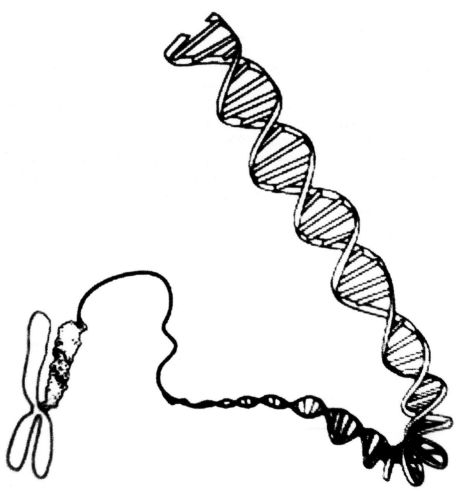

A DNA molecule. (*P.G. de Loriol*)

There have been some notable successes in the use of DNA in 'Cold Cases'. One particular case was that of the murder of a prominent anti-nuclear campaigner, 78-year-old Hilda Murrell, in 1984. This has recently been solved.

Miss Murrell was battered, stabbed and sexually assaulted, leading to death by hypothermia, in 1984. A semen-stained tissue found in the back bedroom of her house and stains on her slip were kept and were analysed in 2002. The result confounded the various theories that had been bandied about in the 1980s: killed by men of the British intelligence services, dispatched by a right-wing group . . . The truth was more prosaic. A labourer, Andrew George, was arrested in 2002 and his DNA matched the stains on both the tissue and the slip. He had been an inmate of a children's home at the time, was bored and had decided to have some fun. He was imprisoned for fourteen years.

In another case, that of the Sarah Payne murder inquiry, a single hair found in the suspect's van was found to match Sarah's DNA profile. Between December 2000 and November the following year a forensic science team carried out 461 microspectrophotometry tests, 23 infrared spectroscopy tests and 128 thin-layer chromatography tests. Roy Whiting was found guilty of murder and sentenced to life imprisonment in 2001.

Strathclyde's police figures also show that they have solved more than 5,000 crimes since the introduction of DNA profiling fifteen years ago. Some of the major murder investigations in the UK, specifically South London, have been notably successful, largely owing to DNA profiling.

DNA profiling has its detractors. A largely political slant, on what could be termed as the most revolutionary statistical tool, has evolved. Could the world's largest DNA database be used not to classify the criminal but to classify the whole of the population in the British Isles? George Orwell's world may be just around the corner.

BIBLIOGRAPHY AND SOURCES

GENERAL

Herber, Mark, *Criminal London*, Phillimore, 2002
Inwood, Stephen, *A History of London*, Macmillan, 1998
Lane, Brian, *The Encyclopedia of Forensic Science*, BCA, 1992
Margary, Harry (ed.), *The A–Z of Victorian London*, Harry Margary, 1987
William, Harry, *South London*, Robert Hale Ltd, 1949

1. DEATH OF A SAINT

Benedictine Monks of St Augustine's, *The Book of Saints*, A. & C. Black,
   1966
Jennings, Charles, *Greenwich*, Little, Brown & Co., 1999
Shaw, Frances, *Osbern's Life of Alphege*, St Paul's Publishing, 1999
Walford, Edward, *Old and New London*, Cassell & Co., 1898

2. DEATH AND DRAMA IN DEPTFORD

Hopkins, Lisa, *Christopher Marlowe, A Literary Life*, Palgrave
   Macmillan, 2000
Nicholl, Charles, *The Reckoning, the Murder of Christopher Marlowe*,
   University of Chicago Press, 1995
Walford, Edward, *Old and New London*, Cassell & Co., 1898

3. STAND AND DELIVER

London Borough of Lambeth Archives Minet Library
O'London, John, *London Stories*, T.C. & E.C. Jack, 1904
The Newgate Annals
Whichelow, Clive, *Local Highwaymen*, Enigma Publishing, 2000

4. THE DULWICH LONER

Herber, Mark, *Criminal London*, Phillimore, 2002
London Borough of Southwark Archives
Loriol, Peter de, *Famous and Infamous Londoners*, Sutton Publishing, 2004

5. A COUNT OF SOME ACCOUNT

The Courier, 23 and 24 July 1812
Duckworth, Colin, *The d'Antraigues Phenomenon*, Avero Publications Ltd, 1986
Godechot Jacques, *Le Comte d'Antraigues, Un Espion dans l'Europe des Emigrés*, Pamphlet, 1985
Journal de L'Empire, 13 August 1812
Loriol, Peter de, *Famous and Infamous Londoners*, Sutton Publishing, 2004
Moniteur Universel, 15 August 1812
The St James Chronicle, 21, 22, 23 and 28 July 1812
The Times, 23 and 28 July 1812

6. THE LAMBETH MURDER

London Borough of Lambeth Archives, Minet Library

7. THE PINE-APPLE TOLL GATE MURDER

London Borough of Lambeth Archives, Minet Library
London Borough of Westminster Archives
O'Sullivan, Kevin, *Dial 'M' for Maida Vale*, Westminster City Archives, 2000
Rayner, J.L. and Cro, G.T., *The Complete Newgate Calendar*, Navarre Society, 1926
Williams, C.A.J., *Greenacre, or the Edgware Road Murder*, printed by Thomas Richardson, pamphlet

8. WHEN IRISH EYES ARE SMILING

Feret, C.J., *Fulham Old and New*, Leadenhall Press, 1900
London Borough of Wandsworth, Local History Studies, Battersea Library
Walford, Edward, *Old and New London*, Cassell & Co., 1898

9. ALL THAT GLISTERS IS NOT GOLD

Downie, R. Angus, *Murder in London*, Arthur Barker, 1973
Fido, Martin, *Murder Guide to London*, Weidenfeld & Nicolson, 1986
Herber, Mark, *Criminal London*, Phillimore, 2002
Lane, Brian, *The Encyclopedia of Forensic Science*, BCA, 1992
The Times, 14 November 1849
Walford, Edward, *Old and New London*, Cassell & Co., 1898

10. WALWORTH MAYHEM

Cavan Observer, 4 August 1860
Curiosities of Street Literature, Reeves & Turner, 196 Strand, 1871
Rayner, J.L. and Cro, G.T., *The Complete Newgate Calendar*, Navarre
  Society, 1926
The Times, 11 and 18 August 1860

11. THE BRIXTON BABY FARMERS

Daily Telegraph, 12 December 1870
Hewitt, Margaret, *Wives and Mothers in Victorian Industry*, Greenwood
  Press Reprint, 1975
Illustrated Police News, 8 and 15 October 1870
Pall Mall Gazette, 31 January 1868
South London Press, 24 September 1870, 8, 15 and 29 October 1870
The Times, 2 and 14 July 1870, 21 and 23 September 1870, 12 October 1870

12. LOVERS' LANE MURDER

Logan, Guy H.B., *Guilty or Not Guilty*, Duffield & Co., 1929
Smith-Hughes, Jack, *Unfair Comment upon some Victorian Murder
  Trials*, Cassell, 1951
The Times, 9 May 1871, 2 June 1871

14. THE MADNESS OF DR MINOR

Murray, K.M. Elizabeth, *Caught in the Web of Words: James Murray and
  the OED*, Yale University Press, 1995
South London Chronicle, 24 February 1872
Winchester, Simon, *The First Meeting between James Murray and William
  Chester Minor: Some New Evidence*, Oxford English Dictionary, June 1998
Winchester, Simon, *The Professor and the Madman*, Harper Perennial,
  New York, 1998

15. THE BALHAM TRAGEDY

Bridges, Yseult, *How Charles Bravo Died*, Jarrolds Ltd, 1956
Hall, Sir John, *The Bravo Mystery*, Bodley Head Ltd, 1923
Lowndes, Mary Adelaide, *What Really Happened?*, Hutchinson, 1926
Penny Illustrated Paper, 22 July 1876

16. STARVED TO DEATH

Attlay, J.B. (ed.), *Trial of the Stauntons*, Notable British Trial Series,
  William Hodge & Co., 1952

Clarke, Sir Edward, *Public Speeches*, George Routledge & Sons, 1894
Police News, 'Harriet Staunton, the Life and Portraits of the Four
  Prisoners Connected with the Penge Case', 21 October 1877

17. THE RICHMOND MYSTERY

Daily News, 9 April 1879
Daily Telegraph, 27 January 1879
Lloyds Weekly, 27 April 1879
O'Donnell, Elliot, *Trial of Kate Webster*, William Hodge & Co., 1925
Penny Illustrated Paper, 5 April 1879, 26 and 29 July 1879

18. RUN FOR THE MONEY

Adam, H.L., *The Trial of George Lamson*, Notable British Trials Series,
  William Hodge & Co., 1951
Hardwick, Michael, *Doctors on Trial*, Herbert Jenkins, 1961
St Aubyn, Giles, *Infamous Victorians*, Constable, 1971
Williams, Montagu, *Leaves of a Life*, Macmillan, 1890

19. TRUST ME, I'M A DOCTOR

Hodge, James H. (ed.), *Famous Trials 5*, Penguin Books, 1955
Jenner, Michael; *London Heritage*, Mermaid Books, 1991
Lloyds Weekly Newspaper, 17 April 1892
McLaren, Angus, *Prescription for Murder: The Victorian Serial
  Killings of Dr Thomas Neill Cream*, University of Chicago Press,
  1993
Ryder, Stephen P. and Piper, John A., *Dr Thomas Neill Cream – a paper*

20. DEATH OF A FIANCÉE

Jackson, Alan, *London's Local Railways*, David & Charles, 1978
Sellwood, Arthur and Sellwood, Mary, *The Victorian Railway Murders*,
  David & Charles, 1979
The Times, 12, 13, 16 and 17 February 1897

21. WAS HE, WASN'T HE?

Brophy, John, *The Meaning of Murder*, Whiting and Wheaton, 1966
Evans, Stewart P. and Skinner, Keith, *The Ultimate Jack the Ripper
  Sourcebook*, Constable & Robinson, 2000
Glyn Jones, Richard (ed.), *True Crime Through History*, Parragon Books,
  2002
Pall Mall Gazette, 24 March 1903

22. FINGERPRINTING

Beavan, Colin, *Fingerprints*, Fourth Estate, 2002
Lambourne, Gerald, *The Fingerprint Story*, Harrap Ltd, 1984
Rowland, John, *The Finger-Print Man: The Story of Sir Edward Henry*, Lutterworth Press, 1959
Sengoopta, Chandak, *Imprint of the Raj*, Macmillan, 2003
Thorwald, Jurgen, *The Marks of Cain*, Thames & Hudson, 1965

23. YOU'RE FINGERED!

Downie, R. Angus, *Murder in London*, Arthur Barker, 1973
Fido, Martin, *Murder Guide to London*, Weidenfeld & Nicolson, 1986
Glyn Jones, Richard (ed.), *True Crime Through History*, Parragon Books, 2002
Lambourne, Gerald, *The Fingerprint Story*, Harrap Ltd, 1984
Lane, Brian, *The Encyclopedia of Forensic Science*, BCA, 1992

24. WHEN YOU GO DOWN TO THE WOODS ...

Downie, R. Angus, *Murder in London*, Arthur Barker, 1973
Fido, Martin, *Murder Guide to London*, Weidenfeld & Nicolson, 1986
Fletcher Moulton, H. (ed.), *The Trial of Steinie Morrison*, William Hodge & Co., 1922
The Times, 7, 8, 9 and 10 March 1911

25. THE BIRDHURST RISE MYSTERY

Croydon Advertiser, 2 June 1928, 13 July 1929, 10 and 17 August 1929
Graham Hall, Jean and Smith, Gordon D., *The Croydon Arsenic Mystery*, Barry Rose Law Publishers Ltd, 1999
Murder Casebook, 'The Croydon Poisonings', Vol. 53, Marshall Cavendish, 1991
The Times, 7, 28, 30 and 31 October 1929
Whittington-Egan, Richard, *The Riddle of Birdhurst Rise*, Harrap, 1975

26. THE BAPTIST CHURCH MURDER

Downie, R. Angus, *Murder in London*, Arthur Barker, 1973
Fido, Martin, *Murder Guide to London*, Weidenfeld & Nicolson, 1986
Jones, Steve, *When the Lights Went Down*, Wicked Publications, 1995
Lane, Brian, *The Encyclopedia of Forensic Science*, BCA, 1992
The National Archives, Kew

27. LET HIM HAVE IT, CHRIS!

Daily Telegraph, 13 July 1974, 25 January 1983, 21 July 1990, 23 January 1997
Montgomery Hyde, H. (ed.), *The Trial of Craig and Bentley*, Notable British Trials Series, William Hodge & Co., 1954
Parris, John, *Most of My Murders*, Frederick Muller Ltd, 1960
People, 21 September 1971
Trow, M.J., *Let Him Have It, Chris*, Constable, 1990
Yallop, David A., *To Encourage the Others*, W.H. Allen, 1971

28. THE LAW OF MISRULE

Downie, R. Angus, *Murder in London*, Arthur Barker, 1973
Fido, Martin, *Murder Guide to London*, Weidenfeld & Nicolson, 1986
Guardian, 5 January 2006
International Journal of Police Science and Management, Vol. 4, No. 4, 2002
South London Press Archives, 1972–5

29. DNA

Daily Telegraph, 9 April 2005
Forensic Science Publication Scheme, 2002
Guardian, 7 May 2005
Independent, 11 August 2005
Lane, Brian, *The Encyclopedia of Forensic Science*, BCA, 1992
Sun, 6 April 2005

INDEX